General Educational Development Testing Service
A Program of the American Council on Education®

Dear GED Candidate:

Congratulations on taking one of the most important steps of your life—earning a GED credential!

Since 1942, millions of people like you have taken the GED Tests to continue their education, to get a better job, or to achieve a sense of accomplishment.

We are delighted to introduce **Keys to GED® Success: Social Studies**—an invaluable resource to help you pass the GED Social Studies Test. It has been developed through a partnership between the GED Testing Service®– developer of the GED Tests–and Steck-Vaughn, a leading provider of GED test preparation materials and the exclusive distributor of the Official GED Practice Tests.

GEDTS researched the types of skills that GED candidates could focus on to improve their chances of passing the tests. We identified the types of questions and possible reasons that test-takers were missing specific questions on each test and decided to share that information. GEDTS collaborated with Steck-Vaughn to target those skills in a workbook that would benefit present and future GED candidates. The skills targeted in our research are called the **GED® Key Skills**—which is what you'll find in this book. In addition to the **GED Key Skills**, this book includes other important lessons that are needed to pass the GED Social Studies Test.

To help GED teachers, there is a Teaching Tips section included. The tips are written to address teaching strategies for some of the key problem areas that emerged from our research.

As the owner of this book, you can use the Pretest to determine exactly which skills you need to target to pass the test. Once you have completed your study, you can determine whether you are ready to take the GED Social Studies Test by taking an Official GED Practice Test—which follows Lesson 20. The GED Testing Service has developed this practice test as a predictor of the score that you will likely earn on the actual GED Social Studies Test.

Remember that there are four other books in the **Keys to GED Success** series. These other books cover the remaining four GED Tests: Language Arts, Reading, Science, Language Arts, Writing, and Mathematics. All titles in this series are available exclusively from Steck-Vaughn.

We wish you the best of luck on the GED Tests.

Executive Director
GED® Testing Service

September 2008

One Dupont Circle NW, Washington, DC 20036-1193
Telephone: 202/939.9490 Fax: 202/659.8875
www.acenet.edu www.GEDtest.org

STECK-VAUGHN

Keys to GED® SUCCESS

Social Studies

Steck Vaughn™

HOUGHTON MIFFLIN HARCOURT
Supplemental Publishers

www.SteckVaughn.com/AdultEd
800-531-5015

P.CVR ©Visions of America/Joe Sohm/Getty Images; p.7 Courtesy of the National Archives (NWDNS-111-C-CC46331); p.16 ©CORBIS; p.19 ©Victoria and Albert Museum, London/Art Resource; p.21 ©Photodisc/Getty Images; p.28 ©Hulton Archive/Getty Images; p.40 ©Bettmann/CORBIS; p.42 ©Tom Stewart/Corbis; p.45 ©Corbis; p.48 ©Hulton Archive/Getty Images; p.66 ©CORBIS; p.67 ©Hulton Archive/Getty Images; p.68 (left) Courtesy of the Library of Congress; p.68 (right) ©Photodisc/Getty Images; p.69 (left) Courtesy of the Library of Congress; p.69 (right) ©United Press International/Courtesy of the Library of Congress; p.72 ©North Wind Picture Archives; p.82 Cleveland Journal/Courtesy of Ohio Historical Society; p.86 ©Bettmann/Corbis.

ISBN-10:   1-4190-5351-5
ISBN-13: 978-1-4190-5351-1

© 2009 Steck-Vaughn, an imprint of HMH Supplemental Publishers Inc.

Steck-Vaughn is a trademark of HMH Supplemental Publishers Inc.

Official GED® Practice Social Studies Test Form PA © 2001, American Council on Education

Printed in the United States of America.

7 8 9 1429 15 14 13 12

XXXXXXXXXX   C D E F G

4500363714

[Contents]

KEY This symbol indicates *GED® Key Skills* as identified by the GED Testing Service®.

Using This Book

Keys to GED® Success: Social Studies has been prepared by Steck-Vaughn in cooperation with the GED Testing Service®. This book focuses on the thinking and graphic interpretation skills needed to pass the GED Social Studies Test.

This book also identifies the *GED® Key Skills*, which are skills that the GED Testing Service® has pinpointed as those most often missed by test takers who come close to passing the GED Tests. For more information about these skills see *A Message from the GED Testing Service®* at the front of this book.

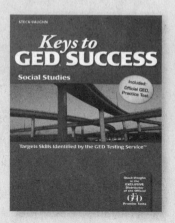

In this book, the *GED Key Skills* are identified by this symbol: **KEY**

It is recommended that students who are preparing to take the GED Tests follow this plan:

1. Take the Social Studies Pretest.
   While it is best to work through all the lessons in this book, students can choose to focus on specific skills. The *Social Studies Pretest* assesses the 20 skills in this book. The *Pretest Performance Analysis Chart* on page 9 will help students to target the skills that need the most attention.

2. Work through the 4-page skill lessons in the book.
   • The first page of each lesson provides an approach to the skill and to thinking through the questions. Students should carefully read the step-by-step thinking strategies and pay attention to the explanations of why the correct answers are right and why the wrong answer choices are incorrect.

   • The second page of each lesson contains sample GED questions. Students should use the hints and the answers and explanations sections to improve their understanding of how to answer questions about each skill.

   • The third and fourth pages of each lesson present GED practice questions that allow students to apply the skill to the same types of questions that they will see on the test.

Students should use the *Answers and Explanations* at the back of this book to check their answers and to learn more about how to make the correct answer choices.

3. Take the *Official GED® Practice Test Form PA: Social Studies* in this book and analyze the results.

The half-length practice test at the end of this book is the Official GED Practice Test Form PA: Social Studies–developed by the GED Testing Service®. Taking this test allows students to evaluate how well they will do on the actual GED Social Studies Test.

Based on the results, test administrators can determine if the student is ready to take the actual test. Those students who are not ready will need more study and should use the other GED Social Studies preparation materials available from Steck-Vaughn, which are listed at the back of this book and can be found at www.SteckVaughn.com/AdultEd.

4. Prior to taking the GED Social Studies Test, take an additional Official GED Practice Test.

The more experience that students have taking practice tests, the better they will do on the actual test. For additional test practice, they can take the Full-Length Practice Test Form or any of the other Official GED Practice Tests available from Steck-Vaughn at www.SteckVaughn.com/AdultEd.

By using this book and the others in this series, students will have the information and strategies developed by both the GED Testing Service® and experienced adult educators, so that they can reach their goal—passing the GED Tests.

Teaching Tips

Below are suggested interactive teaching strategies that support and develop specific **GED₍®₎ Key Skills**.

Make Inferences (Social Studies **KEY** Skill 5)

Discuss the difference between an observation (what you see or read) and an inference (an assumption about what you see or read). Use an everyday example—you are inside and notice that suddenly it gets dark and windy outside (observation); you think that a storm is coming (inference).

- Look at photographs of people in your GED Social Studies text or in other social studies sources.
- Make a list of the details that you see in the pictures (observation).
- Make 3 or more inferences about the photograph, such as, "Who are these people? What are they doing? What is the purpose of including this picture with this information or the article?"

Identify Facts and Opinions (Social Studies **KEY** Skill 6)

Bring newspapers to class over several days. Discuss the differences between factual information in a news story and opinions expressed in editorials and in columns by individuals who present their own ideas on the news of the day.

- Follow a major news story for several days. It can be local, national, or international.
- Locate one or more editorials or commentaries on the event.
- Make a chart with two columns – one with the heading Facts and the other with the heading Opinions. List facts and opinions that you read in the articles.
- Discuss how well (or poorly) an editorial writer or columnist uses facts to support his or her opinions.

Political Cartoons (Social Studies **KEY** Skill 17)

Both the teacher and students can bring in political cartoons from the daily newspaper on a regular basis.

- "Read" all of the information given in a political cartoon, including the characters pictured and any captions or labels. Discuss that all of this information has meaning and is important.
- Understand the use of symbolism (e.g. Uncle Sam stands for the United States) and irony (something that has a different meaning than what is stated) in interpreting the political cartoon.
- Discuss questions, such as: "What do you see in the cartoon? What do the people or objects represent? What is the point that the cartoonist is trying to make? Do you agree or disagree with the cartoonist's opinion? Why?"

Map Skills (Social Studies **KEY** Skill 18)

Locate a U.S. map that contains a compass for directions and has clearly labeled major bodies of water and names of states.

- Locate your own city and state on the map.
- To get a sense of the relative locations of places, students can pose questions to each other, such as: "Nevada is what direction from our state? Are we east or west of the Mississippi? Is our state closer to the Great Lakes than Iowa?"
- This activity can be repeated by locating the U.S. on a world map that has clearly labeled bodies of water and continents.

Content Challenges ....

GED Testing Service₍®₎ research showed that test takers often have difficulty with questions that are based on the following topics. Use your Steck-Vaughn GED Social Studies book to review these concepts.

Basic Economic Concepts – including supply and demand, private or free enterprise, competition, return on investment, and cost/benefit analysis

Geography Concepts – including geographic distributions, concepts, terms, and vocabulary (e.g. equator) and knowledge of basic geographic places and locations (e.g. continents, oceans, etc.)

U.S. History and Government Concepts – including major documents, as well as wars and other conflicts

Social Studies Pretest

Directions

This pretest consists of 20 questions designed to measure how well you know skills needed to pass the GED Social Studies Test. There is one question for each of the 20 lessons in this book.

- Take the pretest and record your answers on the *Pretest Answer Sheet* found on page 123. Choose the <u>one best answer</u> to each question.

- Check your answers in the *Pretest Answers and Explanations* section, which starts on page 105. Reading the explanations for the answers will help you understand why the correct answers are right and why the incorrect answer choices are wrong.

- Fill in the *Pretest Performance Analysis Chart* on page 9 to determine which skills are the most important for you to focus on as you work in this book.

<u>Questions 1 and 2</u> refer to the following table.

Canada: Population by Province / Territory		
Provinces / Territories	Area (sq. mi.)	Population (1996 cen.)
Alberta	255,287	2,696,826
British Columbia	365,948	3,724,500
Manitoba	250,947	1,113,898
New Brunswick	28,355	738,133
Newfoundland	156,649	551,792
Nova Scotia	21,425	909,282
Ontario	412,581	10,753,573
Prince Edward Island	2,185	134,557
Quebec	594,860	7,138,795
Saskatchewan	251,866	990,237
Northwest Territories	503,951	39,672
Yukon Territory	186,661	30,766
Nunavut	818,959	24,730

1. Based on information in the table, which province or territory covers the greatest number of square miles?

   (1) Prince Edward Island
   (2) Ontario
   (3) Quebec
   (4) Nunavut
   (5) Northwest Territories

2. Which of the following can be inferred from the information in the table?

   (1) Canada has a wide diversity of population densities.
   (2) Quebec is the biggest province in Canada.
   (3) The biggest province in Canada also has the largest population.
   (4) The most populous province of Canada is the second largest.
   (5) Only two Canadian provinces have populations over 1 million.

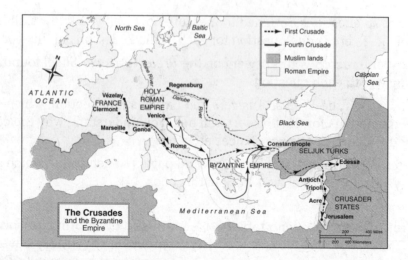

The Crusades were military campaigns by European Christian armies against Muslim territories, primarily as an attempt to capture Jerusalem and save it from the "infidels." The Crusades took place from the eleventh through the fourteenth centuries. The First Crusade succeeded in temporarily occupying four Crusader States, from Antioch south to Jerusalem, but because of infighting and Muslim resistance, these states were never consolidated. In 1204, during the Fourth Crusade, European armies sacked and savagely looted Constantinople. The victors installed a Flemish count as emperor and founded the Latin Empire of Constantinople, which came to an end in 1261, when Muslim troops reentered the city. By that time, the power of the Latin emperors scarcely extended beyond the walls of the city. The Byzantine Empire was reconstituted, but faced threats from the West and from Turkey. Finally, in 1453, Constantinople was conquered by the Turks, who founded the Ottoman Empire. The Byzantine Empire was no more.

3. According to the map, which of the following best describes the general route of the Crusaders?

   (1) The Crusaders' route went through Constantinople.
   (2) The First Crusade temporarily occupied four Crusader States, from Antioch south to Jerusalem.
   (3) The Fourth Crusade traveled by sea from Venice to Constantinople.
   (4) Crusaders embarked from Vézelay, from Venice, and from Regensburg.
   (5) The Crusaders traveled from west to east.

4. Which of the following best summarizes the main idea of the passage?

   (1) The First Crusade made Jerusalem permanently a Crusader State.
   (2) The Crusaders were unable to save Jerusalem from the "infidels."
   (3) The Popes generally did not support the Crusades.
   (4) Constantinople was conquered in 1453.
   (5) The Crusades consolidated the Holy Roman Empire.

5. Which of the following cities became a Crusader state, according to the passage and historical map?

   (1) Rome
   (2) Edessa
   (3) Tripoli
   (4) Constantinople
   (5) Venice

Questions 6 and 7 refer to the following passage about the samurai of Japan.

Samurai were the Japanese warrior class, active from the ninth century until its abolition in 1876. Carefully trained in the martial arts, the samurai were highly effective fighters and expert horsemen.

Bushido, the samurai's way of life, was based on honor and loyalty to the overlord and emperor. Trust, honesty, frugality, and pride were all important samurai values. These values were so important, samurai would commit ritual suicide, known as seppuku, before facing dishonor.

6. Which of the following is implied by the fact that the samurai were an important part of Japanese culture?

(1) The samurai were fierce warriors.
(2) Except for the samurai, most Japanese people were materialistic.
(3) Honor and pride were highly valued in Japan.
(4) When the samurai lifestyle was abolished in 1876, Japanese culture collapsed.
(5) Seppuku was the deepest expression of religious reverence.

7. Based on the passage, what can be concluded about the way the author feels about the samurai?

The author

(1) respects the samurai
(2) dislikes the samurai
(3) doesn't care about the samurai
(4) is undecided about the samurai
(5) feels wary of the samurai

Question 8 refers to the following bar graph.

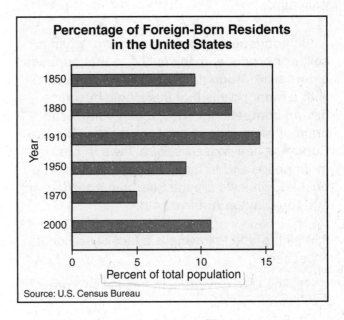

Source: U.S. Census Bureau

8. Which of the following restates information from the bar graph? _Resume / Paraphrase_

(1) Birth rates for immigrants are steadily increasing. _NO_
(2) Immigrants are more accepted now than in the past. _NO_
(3) There were more foreign-born residents in the U.S. in 1910 than at any other time since 1850.
(4) As a percentage of total population, there were more foreign-born residents in the U.S. in 1910 than at any other time since 1850.
(5) Birth rates for immigrants have steadily fallen since 1910.

In economics, a monopoly exists when a seller or producer is the only one that supplies a particular product or service. The problem with a monopoly is that this single business has no competition. Thus, it can control the price of the goods or services it sells. The U.S. Congress has passed several laws to prevent monopolies and to maintain competition. The best known laws are the Sherman Antitrust Act and the Clayton Antitrust Act.

9. Which of the following is a fact based on the passage?

   (1) The U.S. government has laws to prevent monopolies.
   (2) Big business is bad for the economy.
   (3) The U.S. government must regulate business, or it will exploit the consumer.
   (4) The Sherman and Clayton Acts are highly effective laws.
   (5) Monopolies are no longer a problem in the United States because of the Clayton and Sherman Acts.

10. Which of the following restates information from the passage?

   (1) Monopolies have no control over setting prices.
   (2) Monopolies encourage other businesses to compete with their product.
   (3) The U.S. Congress takes a neutral stance when dealing with monopolies.
   (4) Monopolies may cause higher prices, but the product or service is better.
   (5) The U.S. Congress discourages monopolies and encourages competitive pricing.

The term "consumer protection" applies to the efforts of government and public-interest organizations to establish, protect, and enforce the rights of people who buy products or services. Since the 1960s, consumer protection laws have been passed to set safety standards for automobiles, children's clothing and toys, and many household products. Other laws protect consumers from unsafe food and drugs and unfair credit practices. In 1962, President Kennedy articulated four basic rights of consumers: the right to (1) be safe, (2) be informed, (3) choose, and (4) be heard.

11. What assumption does consumer protection make about consumers?

   (1) Consumers are well informed about the goods and services they buy.
   (2) Consumers dislike government intervention.
   (3) Consumers are basically ignorant.
   (4) Consumers alone are responsible for the consumer choices they make.
   (5) Consumers can't always protect themselves.

12. Based on the passage, what would have been one result of the consumer protection laws passed since the 1960s?

   (1) Ralph Nader published *Unsafe at Any Speed*, a critical look at auto safety.
   (2) A fifteen-passenger van is made to be safer than a compact car.
   (3) The U.S. Consumer Product Safety Commission works with foreign manufacturers to make sure they understand the regulations and safety concerns of importing toys into the U.S.
   (4) A government watchdog agency reported in 2008 that 20 percent of the toys made and sold in China in 2008 posed safety risks.
   (5) The U.S. Environmental Protection Agency has programs to protect the nation's water.

Question 13 refers to the following circle graph.

REASONS WOMEN HOLD TWO JOBS

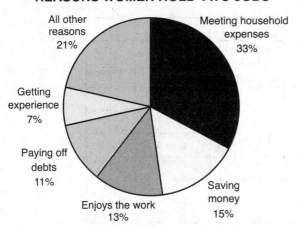

All other reasons 21%

Meeting household expenses 33%

Getting experience 7%

Paying off debts 11%

Enjoys the work 13%

Saving money 15%

Source: Bureau of Labor Statistics

13. Based on information in the circle graph, what is the most likely reason that many women have two jobs?

(1) Many women must pay for their family's everyday needs.
(2) Women are not as well-educated as men.
(3) The male unemployment rate is high among married men.
(4) Most women want to save money for their future.
(5) Women enjoy working additional jobs.

Question 14 refers to the following political cartoon.

14. Eminent domain is a government's right to take private property for public use, usually with compensation to the owner. Which of the following is implied by the cartoon about eminent domain?

(1) Some homeowners are happy to stay put no matter what changes befall their neighborhood.
(2) Most homeowners support eminent domain.
(3) Some homeowners disagree with eminent domain and will fight to resist government's attempts to take their homes.
(4) Eminent domain is unconstitutional.
(5) Eminent domain is unfair to homeowners.

Questions 15 and 16 refer to the following two line graphs.

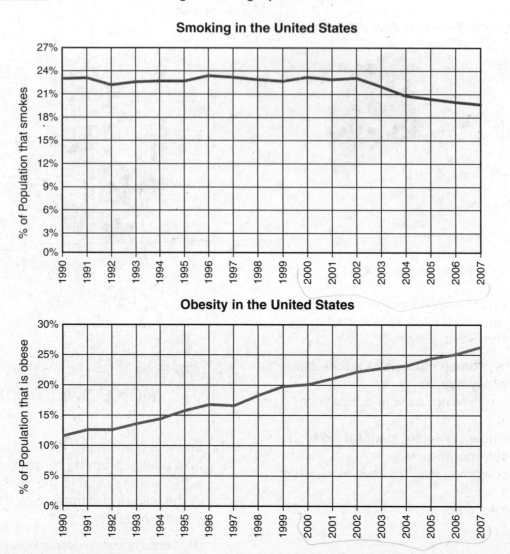

Smoking in the United States

Obesity in the United States

15. Based on the graph that shows obesity rates, which of the following accounts for the steady rise in obesity since 1990?

    (1) Americans are increasingly addicted to fast food and junk food.
    (2) Americans in 2007 spent almost twice as much time in their cars as they did before 1990.
    (3) Most of the population is still not obese.
    (4) The rise in percentage of population that is obese was highest in the period 1997–1998.
    (5) None of the above.

16. Which of the following best restates the information shown in the two graphs for the time period 2000–2007?

    (1) Obesity rates have climbed while smoking rates have remained steady.
    (2) Smoking has increased as obesity rates have climbed.
    (3) Obesity rates have climbed while smoking rates have declined.
    (4) Obesity will lead to higher smoking rates.
    (5) Americans no longer smoke, but they are less fit than ever.

Questions 17 and 18 refer to the following photograph and passage about Vietnam protests.

The war in Vietnam led to both peaceful and violent protests around the United States. On May 4, 1970, members of the Ohio National Guard fired into a crowd of student demonstrators at Kent State University, killing four and wounding nine. For U.S. citizens of all political positions and views, it was one of the low points of the Vietnam era.

17. Based on the photograph and passage, which of the following generalizations is correct?

    (1) Both those who supported the war in Vietnam and those against it were saddened by the Kent State shootings.
    (2) Peaceful protest is never preferable to violent protest.
    (3) Both protestors and police are content to avoid violent confrontation.
    (4) Demonstrations held on sunny days are usually peaceful.
    (5) The demonstrators at Kent State were shot because they "crossed a line" similar to the rope shown in the photo.

18. What does the photograph imply about whether the scene shows a violent or peaceful protest?

    (1) The presence of military police suggests that this is a violent confrontation.
    (2) The girl holding a flower is taunting the military police to make them overreact.
    (3) Nobody seems to know what to do next.
    (4) The girl holding a flower is making a peace offering.
    (5) This is a peaceful protest, with protestors and authorities each calmly holding their ground.

Question 19 refers to the following passage about Miranda rights.

In 1966 the Supreme Court overturned an Arizona court's conviction of Ernesto Miranda. Miranda was initially found guilty of kidnapping and rape. After being identified in a police lineup, Miranda was questioned and then confessed before he was told he had the right to see a lawyer. Because of this, the Supreme Court asserted that Miranda's comments could not be held against him.

A very contentious decision that divided the court, the Miranda case set the precedent for what are now known as Miranda rights. All individuals in police custody must be told they have the right to remain silent, that anything they say can be used against them, and that they have the right to a lawyer. The Supreme Court went further, stating if at any time an individual in custody asks for a lawyer, the police cannot question them any further without a lawyer.

19. Why was Miranda's conviction overturned?

    (1) He was the victim of police brutality.
    (2) He did not commit the crimes.
    (3) He was not informed of his rights.
    (4) He remained silent.
    (5) He was deprived of a lawyer.

Question 20 refers to the following timeline about milestones for women in politics.

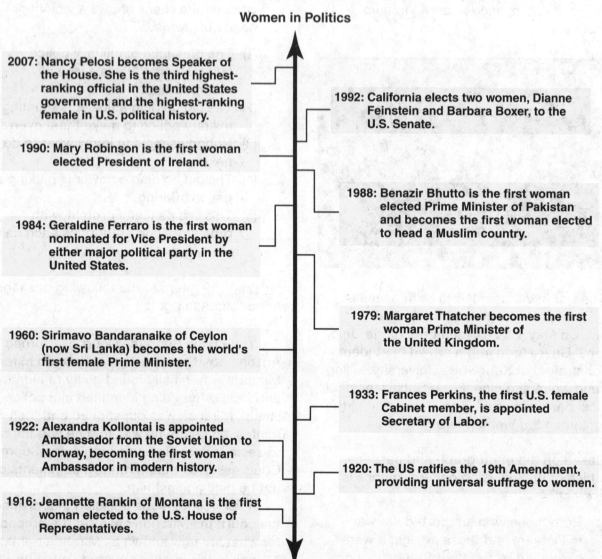

Women in Politics

2007: Nancy Pelosi becomes Speaker of the House. She is the third highest-ranking official in the United States government and the highest-ranking female in U.S. political history.

1992: California elects two women, Dianne Feinstein and Barbara Boxer, to the U.S. Senate.

1990: Mary Robinson is the first woman elected President of Ireland.

1988: Benazir Bhutto is the first woman elected Prime Minister of Pakistan and becomes the first woman elected to head a Muslim country.

1984: Geraldine Ferraro is the first woman nominated for Vice President by either major political party in the United States.

1979: Margaret Thatcher becomes the first woman Prime Minister of the United Kingdom.

1960: Sirimavo Bandaranaike of Ceylon (now Sri Lanka) becomes the world's first female Prime Minister.

1933: Frances Perkins, the first U.S. female Cabinet member, is appointed Secretary of Labor.

1922: Alexandra Kollontai is appointed Ambassador from the Soviet Union to Norway, becoming the first woman Ambassador in modern history.

1920: The US ratifies the 19th Amendment, providing universal suffrage to women.

1916: Jeannette Rankin of Montana is the first woman elected to the U.S. House of Representatives.

20. Which of the following **best** restates information from the timeline?

(1) Women could not run for political office in the United States until after ratification of the 19th Amendment in 1920.

(2) Geraldine Ferraro was the first woman to be elected U.S. President.

(3) Mary Robinson was elected President of Ireland in 1980.

(4) For the first time, California elected two women senators in 1992.

(5) Geraldine Ferraro was the first woman candidate for Vice President of the United States.

Pretest Performance Analysis Chart

The following chart can help you to determine your strengths and weaknesses on the skill areas needed to pass the GED Social Studies Test.

- Use the *Pretest Answers and Explanations* on pages 105–107 to check your answers.
- On the chart below
  - Circle the question numbers that you answered correctly.
  - Put a check mark (✓) next to the skills for which you answered the questions incorrectly.
  - Use the page numbers to find the lessons that you need to target as you work.

Question Number	Skills to Target (✓)	GED Social Studies Skill Lessons	Page Numbers
10		**Skill 1:** Restate Information	10–13
4		**Skill 2:** Summarize Ideas	14–17
6		**Skill 3:** Identify Implications	18–21
12		**Skill 4:** Apply Ideas in a Different Context	22–25
2		**Skill 5:** Make Inferences	26–29
9		**Skill 6:** Identify Facts and Opinions	30–33
11		**Skill 7:** Recognize Unstated Assumptions	34–37
19		**Skill 8:** Identify Causes and Effects	38–41
7		**Skill 9:** Draw Conclusions	42–45
17		**Skill 10:** Evaluate Support for Generalizations	46–49
1		**Skill 11:** Tables and Charts	50–53
8		**Skill 12:** Bar Graphs	54–57
15		**Skill 13:** Line Graphs	58–61
13		**Skill 14:** Circle Graphs	62–65
18		**Skill 15:** Photographs	66–69
20		**Skill 16:** Timelines and Drawings	70–73
14		**Skill 17:** Political Cartoons	74–77
3		**Skill 18:** Maps	78–81
5		**Skill 19:** Combine Text and Graphics	82–85
16		**Skill 20:** Combine Information from Graphics	86–89

Skill 1

Restate Information

Some questions on the GED Social Studies Test will ask you to read a passage or to look at a graphic and then to recognize a **restatement** of some information. When you restate information, you express the same idea in different words. For example, you might read a passage and be asked to identify the same information written a different way.

Read the passage. Choose the <u>one best answer</u> to the question.

Thousands of pioneers traveled by wagon train to settle the open land of the West. But the real growth of the West could not have happened without the railroad. The Union Pacific and Central Pacific Railroads came to an historic meeting on May 10, 1869. Chinese crews laid rails eastward from California while Irish crews worked west from Nebraska. They met in Promontory, Utah, to form the first transcontinental line.

During the next twenty years, the miles covered by railroads increased to over 160,000. Trips that once took three months now took only a week. The number of settlers increased. Wheat and cattle could easily be shipped east to feed the growing number of city dwellers.

QUESTION: Which of the following is the best restatement of the second sentence of the first paragraph?

(1) Workers from Ireland and China built the first transcontinental railway line.
(2) The growth of the railroads and the settlement of the West were inseparable events.
(3) The railroads had an important impact on the culture of the West.
(4) The role of the railroads in settling the West was fairly insignificant.
(5) Railroads made huge profits because of Western settlement.

EXPLANATIONS

STEP 1

To answer this question, ask yourself:

• What is this passage about? <u>The westward expansion of the railroad lines made a significant contribution to the growth of the settlements in that region.</u>
• What is the question asking me to do? <u>Choose the statement that puts the meaning of the second sentence into other words.</u>

STEP 2

Evaluate all the answer choices and choose the <u>best</u> answer.

(1) No. This is referred to later in the first paragraph, but it is not a restatement of the information in the second sentence.
(2) Yes. This is a restatement of, "But the real growth of the West could not have happened without the railroad."
(3) No. Cultural changes are not discussed in the sentence or in the passage at all.
(4) No. This statement contradicts the main point of the sentence.
(5) No. While the railroads did make huge profits, this is not what the sentence is about.

ANSWER: (2) The growth of the railroads and the settlement of the West were inseparable events.

Practice the Skill

Try these examples. Choose the **one best answer** to each question. Then check your answers and the explanations.

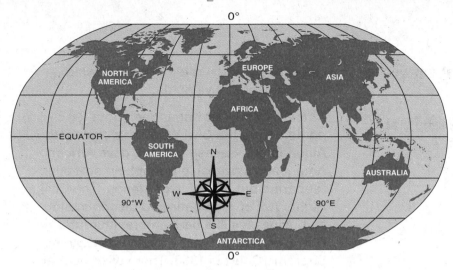

A meridian is a line on a map that runs from north to south. The prime meridian, at 0°, provides a central, fixed point from which the other lines can be measured. The number of degrees and the direction—either east or west of the prime meridian—identify the location of other meridians.

1. Which of the following best describes meridians?

   Meridians are

   (1) imaginary horizontal lines on a map
   (2) lines on a map parallel to the equator
   (3) vertical lines that divide a map into sectors
   (4) lines that divide a map into countries
   (5) lines that divide a map into continents

   HINT Which of the statements defines meridians in different words?

2. Which of the following is a restatement of the information on the map about the equator?

   (1) It is the same as the prime meridian.
   (2) It intersects all of the meridians.
   (3) It runs from north to south on the map.
   (4) It is a part of North America.
   (5) It is south of Australia.

   HINT What happens if you follow the line that is labeled EQUATOR?

Answers and Explanations

1. (3) vertical lines that divide a map into sectors
Meridian lines run north to south, so they are vertical, and they do divide maps into sections (option 3).

Meridians do not run from east to west, or horizontally (option 1), so they are not parallel to the equator (option 2). None of the information in the passage or on the map indicates divisions of countries (option 4) or continents (option 5).

2. (2) It intersects all of the meridians.
Option (2) is correct because the map shows a horizontal line, labeled EQUATOR, that runs across the map and intersects all of the meridians.

Options (1) and (3) are incorrect because the equator runs east to west, and the passage says that all meridians, including the prime meridian, go north to south. Options (4) and (5) are incorrect because the map does not show the equator going through North America or south of Australia.

Restate Information

Directions: Choose the <u>one best answer</u> to each question.

Questions 1 and 2 refer to the following graph about urban and rural populations.

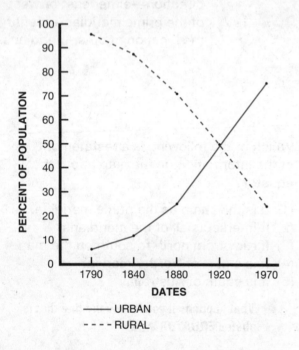

1. Which amount restates the approximate number of people in rural America in 1880?

   (1) 70 people per square mile
   (2) 700 per one million people
   (3) 70 percent of the people
   (4) 70 thousand people
   (5) 70 million people

2. In which year did about half the people in America live in cities?

   (1) 1790
   (2) 1840
   (3) 1880
   (4) 1920
   (5) 1970

Questions 3 and 4 refer to the following passage about civil rights.

African Americans began their fight for civil rights before the Civil War. The Fourteenth Amendment, passed in 1866, gave African Americans citizenship but upheld so-called "separate but equal" segregation. The Civil Rights Act of 1875 outlawed discrimination by businesses like bars and restaurants. However, the 1875 act was reversed by the Supreme Court in 1883. There were no major legal advances in the struggle for civil rights until 1954, when the Supreme Court outlawed "separate but equal" schools in *Brown vs. the Board of Education.*

3. Which of the following is a restatement of the last sentence?

   (1) *Brown vs. the Board of Education* was the last advance in civil rights.
   (2) Between 1883 and 1954, there were no major legal advances in civil rights.
   (3) By 1954, all forms of discrimination had been outlawed.
   (4) African Americans no longer fight for civil rights.
   (5) Marches were the most effective means of protest.

4. From the passage, what can you say African Americans gained from civil rights reforms of the 1950s and beyond?

   (1) the end of racial profiling
   (2) freedom from slavery
   (3) American citizenship
   (4) the right to own property
   (5) the end of "separate but equal" education

> **TIP**
>
> To recognize a restatement, decide which of the answer choices is another way of stating information in the passage or graphic.

Questions 5 and 6 refer to the map and passage on evolution of the continents.

Evolution of the continents

200 Million Years Ago

LAURASIA

GONDWANALAND

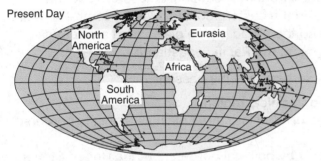

Present Day

North America

Eurasia

Africa

South America

According to the theory of continental drift, the shapes and positions of the continents have evolved over hundreds of millions of years. This theory is based partly on the fact that the shapes of the continents could fit together almost like pieces in a jigsaw puzzle. The theory of drifting continents, as well as the shifting plates on which the continents sit, explains how mountains, volcanoes, and other physical features of Earth have come about.

5. Which of the following statements most accurately restates the theory represented in the passage and map?

(1) Our modern maps are not accurate.
(2) The shapes of the continents have developed gradually during Earth's history.
(3) Eventually, the continents will fit together like pieces in a jigsaw puzzle.
(4) Modern mapmakers must consider the ever-changing nature of Earth's surface.
(5) Millions of years ago, Earth had less ocean and more landmass.

6. How could you best restate the information presented in the first map?

(1) Earth's continents have always looked the way they do today.
(2) The continents are drifting apart at a rapid pace.
(3) All of Earth's land was once clustered together.
(4) The oceans are pushing the continents apart.
(5) The continents of today have unclear borders.

Question 7 refers to the following chart.

Fastest-Growing Jobs, 2006–2016
1. Network systems and data communications analysts
2. Personal and home care aides
3. Home health aides
4. Computer engineers
5. Veterinary technologists and technicians
Sources: *Bureau of Labor Statistics; Occupational Outlook Handbook*

7. Which of the following restates the information about the fastest-growing jobs?

The fastest growing job categories are in

(1) computer-related and health care industries
(2) veterinary medicine
(3) the southwestern United States
(4) the Bureau of Labor Statistics
(5) India and China

Answers and explanations start on page 109.

Skill 2

Summarize Ideas

Some questions on the GED Social Studies Test will ask you to **summarize** the **main idea** of a passage or graphic. A summary does not include every detail, but it does state the meaning, intent, and main points of the original source.

Read the passage. Choose the <u>one best answer</u> to the question.

The United States can be defined by its geographic borders. It extends across North America from the Atlantic Ocean to the Pacific Ocean. It also extends from the Canadian border in the north to the Gulf of Mexico and the Mexican border in the south.

The United States is naturally divided into three sections: an eastern section, including the Appalachian Mountains and the eastern coastal plain; a central section, including the Mississippi River basin and the broad prairie plains; and a western section, including the Rocky Mountains and the Pacific coastlands.

QUESTION: Which of the following <u>best</u> summarizes the passage?

(1) The United States has three geographical regions.
(2) The United States, which can be divided into three main sections, is bordered by both land and oceans.
(3) Some countries are defined solely by political borders, but the United States is defined by geographic borders.
(4) The United States is a vast country stretching from one ocean to another.
(5) The geographic border of the United States can keep its three sections safe from attack.

EXPLANATIONS

STEP 1 To answer this question, ask yourself:

- What is this passage about? <u>The United States can be defined by its geographic borders, and the country's geography can be divided into three main sections.</u>
- What is the question asking me to do? <u>Choose the summary statement that best states the main points of the passage.</u>

STEP 2 Evaluate all the answer choices and choose the best answer.

(1) No. This option summarizes only the ideas in the second paragraph of the passage.
(2) Yes. This option best summarizes the main ideas of both paragraphs without including unnecessary details.
(3) No. While the passage indicates the U.S. can be defined by its geographic borders, the passage does not mention or suggest that some countries are defined solely by political borders.
(4) No. While correct, this option summarizes only the second sentence of the first paragraph.
(5) No. Safety from attack is not mentioned in the passage, so this option is not a summary.

ANSWER: (2) The United States, which can be divided into three main sections, is bordered by both land and oceans.

Practice the Skill

Try these examples. Choose the <u>one best answer</u> to each question. Then check your answers and the explanations.

Experts believe that more than 10,000 years ago, during a great ice age, a bridge of land connected Siberia and Alaska. According to the theory, this bridge provided the pathway for the first people to come to North America. Once across, these people, referred to as Paleo-Indians, found narrow ice-free corridors that offered a route south.

Migration Route from Asia to the Americas 12,000 – 20,000 Years Ago

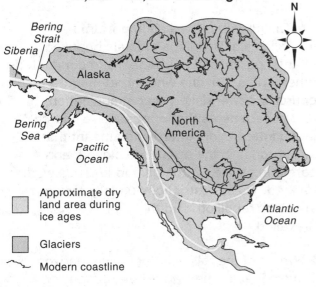

Approximate dry land area during ice ages

Glaciers

Modern coastline

1. Which of the following <u>best</u> summarizes the map and passage?
   - (1) Christopher Columbus did not discover America.
   - (2) The first North Americans faced many challenges.
   - (3) The living conditions for Paleo-Indians were hard and many did not survive.
   - (4) North America has changed since the Ice Age.
   - (5) The first North Americans probably came over a land bridge from Siberia.

   HINT Which statement expresses the main ideas in the map and passage?

2. Which statement <u>best</u> summarizes the information from the map about much of North America?
   - (1) It was once covered by glaciers.
   - (2) It was once covered by water.
   - (3) It was home to many people.
   - (4) People could not survive there.
   - (5) It was inhabited by people who migrated from the south.

   HINT What does the map tell about conditions in North America during the Ice Age?

Answers and Explanations

1. (5) The first North Americans probably came over a land bridge from Siberia.
Option (5) is correct. The map shows the possible migration route from Asia to the Americas during a great ice age. The land bridge route is the main idea of the passage.

Neither the map nor the passage mentions Christopher Columbus (option 1). While the Paleo-Indians and their route south are mentioned, their challenges (option 2) and living conditions (option 3) are not. While it is true that North America has changed since the Ice Age (option 4), this is not the subject of the map or passage.

2. (1) It was once covered by glaciers.
Option (1) is correct because the map shows that the majority of North America was covered by glaciers during a great ice age.

Option (2) is incorrect because, according to the map, North America was not covered by water. Options (3) and (4) are incorrect because the map does not give information about population numbers or climate. Option (5) is incorrect because, as the map demonstrates, migration came from the north and west.

Summarize Ideas

Directions: Choose the <u>one best answer</u> to each question.

<u>Question 1</u> refers to the following cartoon and passage about the Supreme Court.

Before the Civil War, the Supreme Court heard about 300 cases per year. By 1885, the year the cartoon above was published, the court heard over 1,300 cases per year. Six years later, Congress created the circuit appeals courts to ease the burden on the Supreme Court.

1. Which of the following <u>best</u> summarizes the main ideas of the cartoon and the passage?

   (1) Very few legal cases were tried before the Civil War.
   (2) The Supreme Court justices were men.
   (3) Congress created the Circuit Court of Appeals.
   (4) People looked to the Supreme Court to solve their problems.
   (5) The Supreme Court was overworked.

> **TIP**
>
> A summary statement must be broad enough to represent all the information given in the supporting details, and it must be consistent with those details.

<u>Questions 2 and 3</u> refer to the following passage about the church during the Middle Ages.

The church held Western Europe together during the Middle Ages. The dominant force in the region at the time, the church became a major part of medieval government. The church maintained courts, provided resting points for travelers, and even served as hospitals.

The church played an important role in civilian life. Religious officials baptized infants, performed marriages, and conducted funeral rites. Anyone who threatened the church's power risked excommunication, and governments that opposed the church faced interdiction. Interdiction meant that all churches in the area were closed, and ceremonies like weddings and funerals were banned. These restrictions usually resulted in citizen rebellion, and the church usually prevailed.

2. Which of the following <u>best</u> summarizes the main idea of the second paragraph?

   (1) Everyone in medieval Europe believed in God.
   (2) Churches were built in every town.
   (3) The churches were controlled by feudal lords.
   (4) Those who threatened the church risked excommunication.
   (5) The church controlled many aspects of everyday life.

3. Which of the following statements <u>best</u> summarizes the full passage?

   (1) The church was the most powerful force in medieval Europe.
   (2) Church officials performed funerals.
   (3) The church controlled many aspects of everyday life.
   (4) Everyone was extremely pious.
   (5) Everyone was required to go to church.

Questions 4 and 5 refer to the following chart and passage about the Supreme Court.

Associate Justices of the U.S. Supreme Court, 2008	
Justice	Date Sworn In
John Paul Stevens	1975
Antonin Scalia	1985
Anthony M.Kennedy	1988
David H. Souter	1990
Clarence Thomas	1991
Ruth Bader Ginsburg	1993
Stephen G. Breyer	1994
Samuel A. Alito, Jr.	2006

When the Supreme Court is seated on the bench to hear cases, Chief Justice John Roberts sits in the center. The eight Associate Justices are seated to his right and left in order of seniority. The senior Associate sits to the right of Chief Justice Roberts, the next senior Associate sits to his left, the next to his right, and so forth, alternating right to left.

4. Which of the following best summarizes the passage?

   (1) Seating arrangements on the Supreme Court follow a formal pattern based on length of time of service on the Court.
   (2) Seating on the Supreme Court is very complex.
   (3) Chief Justice Roberts is the head of the U.S. Supreme Court.
   (4) The individuals who serve on the Supreme Court are constantly changing.
   (5) Seating on the Supreme Court changes often.

5. Based on the information, which of the Associate Justices sits the farthest to the left of the Chief Justice?

   (1) Justice Stevens
   (2) Justice Breyer
   (3) Justice Alito
   (4) Justice Kennedy
   (5) Justice Souter

Questions 6 and 7 refer to the following passage about the Viking age.

The Viking age is defined by the Viking raids, which lasted from the year 795 to 1066. During that period Scandinavian warriors traveled extensively throughout Europe.

Several theories attempt to explain the beginning and rapid expansion of Viking culture. One theory states that the Vikings were responding to political oppression. Another hypothesis is that overcrowding sent the Vikings searching for new lands.

Regardless of the cause, travel and exploration would have been impossible without the Vikings' technologically advanced ships. Their shallow draft-keeled ships could sail in water as shallow as three feet. More importantly, the ships were fast and able to travel to Iceland from Norway in just one week. The Vikings could reach other points in Europe much faster by sea than over land.

The Vikings had an important impact on Europe. Europe's maritime knowledge and technology, legal systems, land use, and emigration were all advanced because of the Vikings.

6. Based on the passage, what was a benefit of Viking influence?

   (1) raids
   (2) overcrowding
   (3) maritime technology
   (4) trade
   (5) cultural diversity

7. What is the best summary of paragraph 3?

   (1) The Vikings perfected overland travel.
   (2) Ships were crucial to Viking success.
   (3) Vikings loved to travel.
   (4) Vikings could travel to Iceland in one week.
   (5) Many theories explain why the Viking raids began.

Answers and explanations start on page 109.

Comprehension

Identify Implications

Questions on the GED Social Studies Test may ask you to identify the implications of information contained in passages or graphics. An **implication** is an idea that is conveyed or suggested without being directly stated. When trying to identify implications, evaluate the ideas and information that are stated directly and consider the situation or circumstance. You can also use what you know of the world to identify implications.

Read the passage. Choose the <u>one best answer</u> to the question.

According to its classic definition, capitalism has four characteristics. First, the land and capital used to produce goods and services are privately owned. Second, economic activity occurs through markets where buyers and sellers interact. Third, those who own the land and capital and those who work for them are all free to pursue their own self-interests and to seek maximum gain. Fourth, minimal government supervision is required because competition in the market ensures the greatest good for the entire society.

Of the world's nations, the United States conforms most closely to this ideal model of capitalism. However, the U.S. government still supervises many details of economic activity, especially since the Great Depression, when U.S. capitalism seemed in danger of collapse.

QUESTION: Based on the passage, which of the following statements is an implication about the role of government in U.S. capitalism?

   (1) Governmental involvement has always been essential.
   (2) Government has no business interfering in the economy.
   (3) The need for government involvement changes with circumstances.
   (4) U.S. voters determine the extent of government involvement.
   (5) A capitalist economy is totally independent of government involvement.

EXPLANATIONS

STEP 1 To answer this question, ask yourself:

- What is this passage about? <u>the four characteristics of capitalism and U.S. conformity to the ideal model</u>
- What is the question asking me to do? <u>Identify unstated information in the passage.</u>

STEP 2 Evaluate all the answer choices, and choose the best answer.

   (1) No. Governmental involvement is a reaction to changing circumstances.
   (2) No. This passage gives no implication that government should not interfere in the economy. This also contradicts the fourth characteristic.
   (3) Yes. U.S. government involvement changed after the Great Depression and continues to respond as needed to changes in economic circumstances.
   (4) No. The passage implies nothing about how government involvement is determined.
   (5) No. This statement contradicts the passage. It is not implied.

ANSWER: (3) The need for government involvement changes with circumstances.

Practice the Skill

Try these examples. Choose the **one best answer** to each question. Then check your answers and the explanations.

<u>Questions 1 and 2</u> refer to the passage and painting below.

The Great Wave at Kanagawa is a painting created during Japan's Edo period. Hard to see are fishing boats braving the storm to transport their catch to shore. In the background is Mount Fuji, Japan's most important spiritual site.

1. From the painting and passage above, what is an important implication about Japanese culture?

   (1) Japanese people fish primarily for fun.
   (2) Japanese people revere the sea more than Mount Fuji.
   (3) In Japan the sea represents an angry deity.
   (4) The Japanese have close spiritual and economic ties to the sea.
   (5) Japanese fishers feel isolated from the rest of Japanese society.

   HINT What aspect of Japanese culture is suggested in the painting?

2. What is the implication of the fishing boats shown in the painting?

   The boats

   (1) warn against going out in storms
   (2) symbolize the foolishness of fishing in the sea
   (3) show the courage of the people who fish
   (4) add an element of suspense
   (5) remind viewers that fishing is a good leisure activity

   HINT What did the artist communicate about Japanese culture by including the fishing boats in the print?

Answers and Explanations

1. (4) The Japanese have close spiritual and economic ties to the sea.

The painting's display of fishing boats braving a storm, with Mount Fuji in the background, implies that the sea is of spiritual and economic importance to the Japanese (option 4).

That the Japanese fish mainly for fun (option 1), respect the sea more than Mount Fuji (option 2), or that the sea is symbolic of an angry god or goddess (option 3) are not suggested by the painting or passage. The feelings of the Japanese fishers (option 5) are not implied by the passage or painting.

2. (3) show the courage of the people who fish

Option (3) is correct because the fishermen must be brave to navigate such rough seas.

Option (1) is incorrect because the painting does not convey a warning. Option (2) is incorrect because the painting does not suggest fishing is foolish. While the painting may provide suspense (option 4) by making us wonder if the huge waves will harm the vessels, this is an effect, not an implication. The painting does not imply fishing is a leisure activity (option 5).

Identify Implications

Directions: Choose the one best answer to each question.

Questions 1 through 4 refer to the following graph about population change.

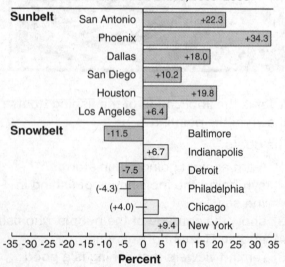

Population Change for the Six Largest Sunbelt and Snowbelt Cities, 1990–2000

1. Which of the following statements **best** summarizes the information from the table?

   (1) The population of the largest sunbelt cities grew, with Phoenix showing the largest increase.
   (2) The populations of the six largest sunbelt cities grew at about the same rate.
   (3) The population in the sunbelt is shifting from Houston to San Diego.
   (4) The population of San Diego is now larger than that of Los Angeles.
   (5) The populations of sunbelt cities are growing because people want to live in warm climates.

> **TIP**
>
> To identify an implication, you must understand the literal meaning—that is, the stated facts and ideas. Then ask yourself, "What do all the facts and ideas point toward or add up to?"

2. Which of the following implications is **best** supported by the graph?

   (1) Each type of city experienced growth during the 1990s.
   (2) Each type of city experienced a decline in growth during the 1990s.
   (3) Sunbelt cities experienced overall growth in the 1990s, while snowbelt cities experienced an overall drop in population.
   (4) All sunbelt cities experienced a similar amount of growth.
   (5) Snowbelt cities experienced growth in the 1980s.

3. Which of the following statements is implied by the graph?

   (1) The populations of the six largest snowbelt cities declined.
   (2) The city of Detroit was more popular than the city of Indianapolis.
   (3) Population growth in the six largest sunbelt cities was a trend in the 1990s.
   (4) Sunbelt cities have more affordable housing than snowbelt cities.
   (5) The snowbelt population shifted from Detroit to Indianapolis.

4. Based on the graph, which of the following statements is an implication about population growth in urban areas?

   (1) It is stable and unchanging.
   (2) It can increase and decrease.
   (3) It is declining.
   (4) It is shifting from urban to suburban areas.
   (5) It is happening at a faster rate than ever before.

The Gupta dynasty initiated a great literary and scientific age in India. During this period, from about A.D. 320 to 550, much of India's most famous works of poetry and prose were written both in Sanskrit, India's sacred language, and Tamil, the major popular language of southern India. In addition to literature and drama, the people of India made great strides in science. They calculated the circumference of the globe, understood abstract mathematical concepts, and made advances in astronomy and medicine.

5. What does the passage imply about the Gupta dynasty?

(1) The Gupta dynasty covered a wide area.
(2) The Gupta dynasty was a period of ignorance and superstition.
(3) The Guptas valued learning.
(4) Scientists were able to calculate the globe's circumference.
(5) Poets produced some of India's most famous verse.

6. What is implied by the fact that literature was written in both Sanskrit and Tamil?

(1) During the Gupta dynasty, many people were illiterate.
(2) Indians who lived during the reign of the Guptas were bilingual.
(3) Poetry, especially when written in Tamil, was unimportant.
(4) Only scientists and religious leaders could read.
(5) Literature was intended for the enjoyment of all classes of society.

7. What does the photograph imply about the Great Wall of China?

(1) Special machines must have been used to build the Great Wall of China.
(2) The Chinese have always possessed superior technology.
(3) The Chinese were so powerful that they were not worried about invasion.
(4) Chinese engineers were able to construct the entire wall without relying on a sophisticated system of mathematics.
(5) The Great Wall of China is a massive structure.

Answers and explanations start on page 110.

Application

Apply Ideas in a Different Context

Some questions on the GED Social Studies Test will ask you to read a passage or look at a graphic and **apply** the ideas to a different **context**, or situation. When you apply ideas in a different context, you use your own knowledge and ideas and apply what you know. For example, you could read about a development in the economy and be asked to apply that information to a specific company's decisions about hiring and firing, as in the question below.

Read the passage. Choose the <u>one best answer</u> to the question.

In economics, permanent loss of one's job is referred to as displacement or dislocation. Workers lose jobs virtually every day as their employers go out of business, move, or reorganize. In today's economic climate, however, mass layoffs, also known as downsizing, have been making headlines. Corporate executives say that downsizing is necessary in our world of global competition and fast-changing technology. Their goal is to create lean, flexible organizations with innovative employees who work in teams that can respond to changing customer needs.

QUESTION: A telecommunications company is preparing to downsize in order to compete in the global economy. Which of the following types of employees are most likely to keep their jobs?

Employees who

(1) have done the same job for many years and know that set of skills very well
(2) have a range of skills that can be used in different departments
(3) are at their best when working independently
(4) have a few specialized skills
(5) are willing to accept lower wages

EXPLANATIONS

STEP 1 To answer this question, ask yourself:

- What is this passage about? <u>Companies say that they lay off workers to get a smaller workforce that can better compete in the global marketplace.</u>
- What is the question asking me to do? <u>Apply the general information about downsizing to the employees of a specific company.</u>

STEP 2 Evaluate all of the answer choices and choose the <u>best</u> answer.

(1) No. These workers would probably not be able to meet changing needs.
(2) **Yes. Workers with a range of skills would be able to respond to changing needs and do a variety of tasks, which would be very valuable to this company.**
(3) No. These workers are not team players; this need is stressed in the passage.
(4) No. A competitive situation requires employees who can do many different things.
(5) No. While some companies would want to pay low wages, this is not the purpose of the downsizing as described in the passage.

ANSWER: (2) have a range of skills that can be used in different departments

Practice the Skill

Try these examples. Choose the <u>one best answer</u> to each question. Then check your answers and read the explanations.

According to the U.S. Constitution, Article II, Section 2, "The President . . . may require the Opinion, in writing, of the principal Officer in each of the executive Departments, upon any Subject relating to the Duties of their respective Offices. . . ."

Historically, the heads of most of the 15 executive departments have been called secretaries; for example, the Secretary of Defense heads up the department that oversees the armed forces. Together, the heads of the departments are called the President's Cabinet. This chart shows some of the departments in the executive branch and their functions.

Executive Department	Function	Head
Commerce	Economic development	Secretary of Commerce
Justice	Law enforcement	Attorney General
State	Foreign policy development	Secretary of State
Treasury	Promoting economic prosperity and financial security	Secretary of the Treasury
Education	Fosters educational excellence	Secretary of Education

1. Which member of the Cabinet deals with our embassies around the world?

   (1) Secretary of State
   (2) Attorney General
   (3) Secretary of Commerce
   (4) Secretary of the Treasury
   (5) Secretary of Education

   HINT Who is the head of the department that deals with international matters?

2. The Justice Department would most likely implement which of the following bills?

   (1) Higher Education Access Act
   (2) Energy Act of 2007
   (3) Economic Stimulus Plan
   (4) Civil Rights Act
   (5) Endangered Species Act

   HINT Which of the bills would be enforced by U.S. law enforcement?

Answers and Explanations

1. (1) Secretary of State
Only the Secretary of State (option 1) deals directly with U.S. foreign activities and policies.

The cabinet members named in options (2) and (5) are not involved in international affairs. Neither the Secretary of Commerce (option 3) nor the Secretary of the Treasury (option 4) are involved in the day-to-day operations of the embassies.

2. (4) Civil Rights Act
Enforcing the Civil Rights Act (option 4) is the only choice that would involve law enforcement—which is the concern of the Justice Department.

The other choices concern issues primarily related to education (option 1), energy (option 2), the economy (option 3), and the environment (option 5).

Apply Ideas in a Different Context

Directions: Choose the one best answer to each question.

Questions 1 and 2 refer to the following chart about job opportunities.

The 10 Fastest Growing Occupations, 1998–2008 (Numbers in thousand of jobs)				
Occupation	Employment		Change	
	1998	2008	Number	Percent
Computer engineers	299	622	323	108
Computer support specialists	429	869	439	102
Systems analysts	617	1,194	577	94
Database administrators	87	155	67	77
Desktop publishing specialists	26	44	19	73
paralegals and legal assistants	136	220	84	62
Personal care and home health aides	746	1,179	433	58
Medical assistants	252	398	146	58
Social and human service assistants	268	410	141	53
Physician assistants	66	98	32	48
Source : Bureau of Labor Statistics				

1. Based on the chart, which of the following fields had the greatest potential for job growth between 1998 and 2008?

    (1) health care
    (2) law
    (3) computer-related
    (4) manufacturing
    (5) human services

2. Which of the following federal departments could make the best use of the data in the graph?

    (1) Department of Justice
    (2) Department of Agriculture
    (3) Department of the Interior
    (4) Department of State
    (5) Department of Labor

Questions 3 and 4 refer to the following passage.

In 1954, the Supreme Court ruled in the case of *Brown v. Board of Education* ". . . that in the field of public education the doctrine of separate but equal has no place. Separate educational facilities are inherently unequal."

3. Which of the following was the basis for the Supreme Court's rulings?

    (1) the First Amendment, which guarantees the right to free speech
    (2) the Fourth Amendment, which guarantees protection against unreasonable searches and seizure
    (3) the Sixth Amendment, which guarantees the right to a speedy trial
    (4) the Tenth Amendment, which reserves powers not delegated to the United States for the states or the people
    (5) the Fourteenth Amendment, which guarantees equal protection under the law for all citizens

4. Which would have been one result of the Supreme Court's ruling?

    (1) providing buses for black and white students to and from integrated public schools
    (2) implementing standardized tests to show educational progress
    (3) lengthening the school day so that all students could achieve more
    (4) eliminating art, music, and physical education classes
    (5) tracking high school students' passing and failure rates

Questions 5 and 6 refer to the following descriptions of different types of maps.

Political maps show the borders of countries, states, territories, and cities.

Historical maps depict events from the past.

Physical maps show landforms and major bodies of water.

Relief maps use shading, color, and contour lines to show the elevations in a particular place.

Road maps show highways, roads, and distances between places.

5. An instructor used a map to show how the armies of Genghis Khan invaded East and Central Asia.

   Which of the following types of maps did he use?

   (1) political
   (2) historical
   (3) physical
   (4) relief
   (5) road

6. A dispatcher from a long-distance freight company plans the delivery route for the trucks.

   Which of the following types of maps does she use?

   (1) political
   (2) historical
   (3) physical
   (4) relief
   (5) road

Question 7 refers to the following map of Maui.

Proposed Area of Resettlement of Native Hawaiians at Kahikinui, Maui

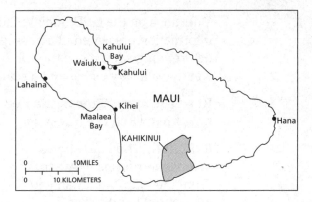

7. Who might use this map of Maui, one of the Hawaiian Islands?

   (1) a committee on population relocation
   (2) a historian
   (3) a photographer looking for mountains and lakes
   (4) a surveyor looking for land elevations
   (5) a tourist driving from Hana to Kihei

8. In U.S. history, the Progressive Era was a period of reform from the 1890s to the 1920s. The Progressives advocated an end to government corruption and sought improvement for workers, women, and citizens in general.

   Which of the following would be a modern-day reflection of the Progressive outlook?

   (1) tax cuts for the wealthy
   (2) limits on workers' rights
   (3) health standards for food production
   (4) improvements to technology
   (5) changes to the driving age

[**TIP**]

To apply ideas in a new context, look at the specifics of each carefully and ask yourself: What is similar? How are they similar?

Answers and explanations start on page 111.

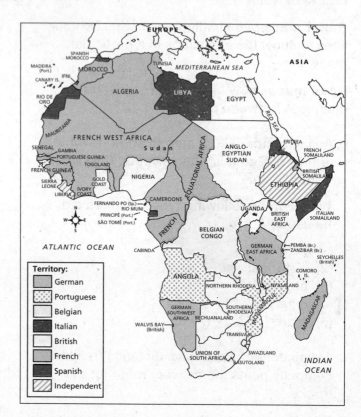

Make Inferences

Questions on the GED Social Studies Test will ask you to **make inferences** about the information presented in a passage or graphic. When making an inference, you are determining what the author or artist is suggesting. For example, if you saw someone wearing a heavy jacket and a scarf, you could infer that it's cold outside.

Read the map. Choose the <u>one</u> <u>best answer</u> to the question.

QUESTION: The map shows colonial territories in Africa. From the map, what can you infer about imperialism?

(1) Africa was highly desirable as a site for colonial settlement.
(2) Ethiopia had no natural resources that would be useful in colonization.
(3) France believed that Africa had no value.
(4) African cultures were not diverse.
(5) Many African countries escaped imperialism.

EXPLANATIONS

STEP 1   To answer this question, ask yourself:

- What is this map about? <u>African countries under the rule of imperialist colonial governments</u>
- What is the question asking me to do? <u>Decide what is suggested by the information in the map.</u>

STEP 2   Evaluate all the answer choices and choose the best answer.

(1) Yes. With so many European countries claiming parts of Africa, it can be inferred that Africa was highly desirable for colonization.
(2) No. The map does not indicate natural resources, so this cannot be inferred.
(3) No. The large areas indicated as French territories clearly contradict the inference that Africa lacked value to France.
(4) No. The map does not address or make suggestions about the diversity of African cultures.
(5) No. The map identified only Ethiopia and Liberia as independent, leading to the inference that only a few countries escaped imperialism.

ANSWER: (1) Africa was highly desirable as a site for colonial settlement.

Practice the Skill

Try these examples. Choose the <u>one best answer</u> to each question. Then check your answers and the explanations.

In its ideal form, socialism has two essential characteristics. First, the goal of economic activity is to fulfill social needs, or the good of society as a whole. The pursuit of private profit is considered immoral. Second, the central government makes the basic economic decisions, such as what to produce, at what price, and for which consumers. By controlling production and distribution, the government can ensure that goods and services flow equitably to the people who need them.

1. From the information in the passage, which of the following statements can be inferred about the role of competition in socialism?

    (1) Government regulation makes competition unnecessary.
    (2) Competition between firms benefits society as a whole.
    (3) Government should encourage competition.
    (4) Competition will lead to private ownership of business, which is the ultimate goal.
    (5) Mild competition benefits society, but intense competition does not.

    HINT What does the passage suggest but not state about competition?

2. Based on the passage, which of the following goals can you infer lies at the heart of socialism?

    (1) private ownership of business
    (2) free enterprise
    (3) minimal interference of government
    (4) fair distribution of wealth
    (5) clear distinctions between economic classes

    HINT What does the passage suggest are the goals of socialism?

Answers and Explanations

1. (1) Government regulation makes competition unnecessary.
Option (1) is correct. When the passage says that government makes the basic economic decisions about products and pricing, it suggests that there is no opportunity or need for competition.

It cannot be inferred from the information in the passage that competition benefits society as a whole (option 2), that government should encourage competition (option 3), or that only mild competition benefits society (option 5). Option (4) is also incorrect; the passage says that private profit is bad, which suggests that private ownership is bad as well.

2. (4) fair distribution of wealth
The emphasis on socialism's discouragement of profit, control of production, and distribution of goods and services suggests that fair distribution of wealth (option 4) is the goal at the heart of socialism.

Option (1) is incorrect because private profit, and therefore private ownership, is considered immoral. The emphasis on government control under socialism suggests that free enterprise (option 2) would be discouraged and contradicts the inference that minimal government involvement (option 3) would be a goal. Option (5) is incorrect because the passage emphasizes that socialism benefits the good of society as a whole, which does not lead to the inference that socialism promotes distinctions based on economic class.

Make Inferences

Directions: Choose the <u>one best answer</u> to each question.

<u>Question 1 and 2</u> refer to the following passage on the age of imperialism.

Imperialism reemerged with the modern nation-state and age of exploration that began in the fifteenth century. As imperialism increased, world powers such as Great Britain and Germany scrambled to control developing nations across the globe. By exploiting the natural resources of other countries, colonizers were able to fuel the industrial revolutions in their homelands.

Countries that embraced imperialism frequently assumed an air of superiority over the populations of the lands they colonized. This behavior was often justified by feelings of paternalism. Known as "the white man's burden," controlling native populations was excused because it was believed that more powerful nations had a divine duty to introduce their colonies to technology, Christianity, and a Western way of life.

1. What does the author suggest about imperialism?

   (1) Imperialism was unfair because both parties did not benefit equally.
   (2) Imperialists felt compelled to formally educate all residents of their colonies.
   (3) Colonized countries benefited from the guidance of their patrons.
   (4) Imperialism always improved the lives of uncivilized people.
   (5) The developing nations were eager to share their natural resources.

> ### TIP
>
> Remember that to make inferences, you must decide which ideas are suggested, not stated directly.

2. What can you infer about the writer's attitude toward the concept of "the white man's burden"?

   The writer

   (1) agrees with the concept
   (2) strongly favors the concept
   (3) feels neutral about the concept
   (4) cares little about the concept
   (5) disapproves of the concept

<u>Questions 3 and 4</u> refer to the following photograph of an engraving.

3. Which group does the engraving suggest is the most powerful?

   (1) the tribal chiefs
   (2) the uniformed white soldiers
   (3) the Africans
   (4) the silent spectators
   (5) both the warriors and the soldiers

4. Based on the picture, you might infer that the white soldiers view Africans

   (1) with respect
   (2) with hatred
   (3) with tolerance
   (4) with disdain
   (5) with admiration

Questions 5 and 6 refer to the following passage about Native Americans and land.

Native Americans differ from the other groups of people in the United States because they lived here and governed themselves long before the U.S. government was established. As self-governing nations, they signed agreements first with colonists and then with the U.S. government. Later, the U.S. government hoped to end conflicts with Native Americans over land by placing them on reservations, which were located in more remote, less desirable areas.

5. Based on the passage, what can you infer about Native Americans?

(1) They were happy to give up their land so that they could be self-governing.
(2) The U.S government did its best to treat them fairly.
(3) They have the same status as other ethnic groups in the United States.
(4) They were forced to give up their best lands to non–Native Americans.
(5) The U.S. government has been able to avoid conflicts with them.

6. Which statement can be inferred from the passage?

(1) Native American culture has benefited from interactions with colonists and the U.S. government.
(2) Native Americans have been victims of the U.S. government's decision to place them on reservations.
(3) Reservations were placed in desirable areas.
(4) Native Americans welcomed the colonists' form of government.
(5) Native American cultures are varied.

Question 7 refers to the following cartoon about the early 1900s.

WORKING MAN

7. What can you infer about the cartoonist's attitude toward the subject of work?

(1) Working people are generally pleased with their jobs.
(2) People will usually follow a strong leader.
(3) Some individuals profit at the expense of other people's work.
(4) Unions were the result of workers' dissatisfaction.
(5) The construction industry was more profitable then than now.

Answers and explanations start on page 111.

Identify Facts and Opinions

Some questions on the GED Social Studies Test will ask you to identify **facts** and **opinions** presented in a passage or graphic. A **fact** is a statement that can be verified, or proven to be true, whereas an **opinion** is a judgment or point of view. Opinions can't be proven to be true.

Read the passage. Choose the <u>one best answer</u> to the question.

The President pushed Congress to use a portion of the budget surplus for tax rebates in 2000. All individuals who paid federal income taxes that same year were eligible for rebates. Married filers received $600, while single taxpayers were sent $300 checks. The money was meant to stimulate the economy and encourage consumer spending. However, the economy sagged into a recession. Most of the rebate money probably went into paying off old debts or into savings accounts. Congress and the President unwisely spent much of the budget surplus on the rebates in a move that did little to benefit the national economy. Despite the lack of success, in February 2008 Congress passed an Economic Stimulus Bill, which provided tax rebate checks to about 117 million middle- and low-income taxpayers, 20 million retirees living on Social Security, and 250,000 U.S. veterans receiving disability benefits.

QUESTION: According to the passage, which of the following is a fact about the tax rebates?

(1) Most individuals probably put their rebates into savings accounts.
(2) People who paid federal income tax received a rebate.
(3) The economy sagged into recession because of the rebates.
(4) Congress shouldn't have approved the Economic Stimulus Bill in 2008.
(5) The rebates really didn't benefit the economy.

EXPLANATIONS

STEP 1 To answer this question, ask yourself:

• What is this passage about? <u>the federal income tax rebates</u>
• What is the question asking me to do? <u>Recognize the facts and opinions in the passage.</u>

STEP 2 Evaluate all the answer choices and choose the best answer.

(1) No. This option is an opinion, not a fact that can be proven.
(2) Yes. The specific conditions established for rebate recipients are facts that can be proven through the historical record.
(3) No. It is true that the economy went into recession, but the reason cannot be proven to be because of the rebates.
(4) No. That Congress shouldn't have approved the stimulus for 2008 is an opinion, not a fact.
(5) No. That the rebates didn't really benefit the economy is an opinion, not a fact.

ANSWER: (2) People who paid federal income tax received a rebate.

Practice the Skill

1. Based on the information in the map, which of the following is an opinion?

   (1) Texas is among the leaders in minority-owned firms.
   (2) The northern plains have few minority-owned firms.
   (3) Many minorities own businesses in Hawaii.
   (4) Arizona has a higher percentage of minority-owned businesses than Vermont.
   (5) North and South Dakota offer very little economic opportunity.

   HINT Which statement cannot be proven from information given in the map?

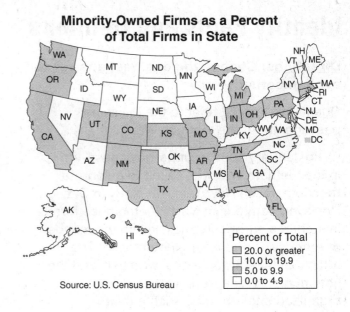

Minority-Owned Firms as a Percent of Total Firms in State

Source: U.S. Census Bureau

Percent of Total
- 20.0 or greater
- 10.0 to 19.9
- 5.0 to 9.9
- 0.0 to 4.9

2. Based on the information in the map, which of the following is a fact?

   (1) Minnesota has few minorities.
   (2) California is the most economically diverse state.
   (3) Florida is the wealthiest state.
   (4) The majority of firms in the U.S. are owned by non-minorities.
   (5) More minorities should own businesses.

   HINT Which statement can be verified from information given in the map?

Answers and Explanations

1. (5) North and South Dakota offer very little economic opportunity.
This is an opinion because it is based on a belief that is not supported by the map. More evidence would be needed to make a factual claim.

That Texas is a leader in percentage of minority-owned firms (option 1), the northern plains have few such firms (option 2) while Hawaii has many (option 3), and Arizona has a higher percentage of such firms than Vermont (option 4) are facts based on the map.

2. (4) The majority of firms in the U.S. are owned by non-minorities.
The map and the key clearly show that most businesses in the United States are owned by non-minorities.

The map does not address Minnesota's minorities (option 1), California's economic diversity (option 2), Florida's wealth (option 3), or who should own businesses (option 5).

Identify Facts and Opinions

Directions: Choose the one best answer to each question.

Questions 1 and 2 refer to the following passage about the Vietnam War.

In January 1968, a three-day cease-fire in the Vietnam War was called to celebrate the Vietnamese New Year, Tet Nguyen Dan. However, communist North Vietnamese forces launched a surprise attack, killing thousands of Americans and South Vietnamese. The attack shocked Americans, who believed the communist forces were neither strong nor organized enough to do such a thing.

Senator Eugene McCarthy responded to the Tet offensive in a speech, saying, "In 1965, we were told the enemy was being brought to its knees. In 1966, 1967, and now again in 1968, we hear the same hollow claims of progress and victory. For the fact is that the enemy is bolder than ever, while we must steadily enlarge our commitment. The Democratic Party in 1964 promised no wider war. Yet the war is getting wider every month."

1. Which of the following is a fact about the broken cease-fire during Tet in 1968?

   (1) It led to the deaths of thousands of Americans and Vietnamese.
   (2) It was a celebration of the New Year.
   (3) Americans weren't surprised.
   (4) The enemy fought on its knees.
   (5) The enemy was bolder than ever.

2. Which of the following is an opinion?

   (1) The Vietnamese New Year is in January.
   (2) The U.S. government continued to make hollow claims of progress and victory.
   (3) The killings of Tet shocked U.S. citizens.
   (4) Communist forces broke the cease-fire.
   (5) Americans and Vietnamese were killed in the Tet offensive.

Questions 3 and 4 refer to the following graph and passage about prison populations.

Number of Prison and Jail Inmates, 1910–2000

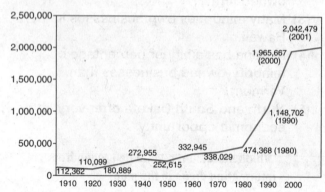

Source: U.S. Department of Justice

Some prisons house more inmates than they were built for. Overcrowding is partly the result of inmates serving longer terms due to a get-tough policy on crime. Despite federal funding to build more prisons, many people believe the situation can only be handled by adding more guards.

3. What fact does the graph reveal to help explain the overcrowding problem in prisons?

   (1) Courts are doing a good job against crime.
   (2) The prison population more than doubled from 1980 to 1990.
   (3) Not enough prisons are being built.
   (4) The crime rate in America is rising.
   (5) More inmates should be paroled.

4. Which of the following is an opinion from the passage?

   (1) Building more prisons will solve the problem.
   (2) The problem can't be solved.
   (3) More guards are needed.
   (4) The situation has not yet become dangerous.
   (5) Prisons are overcrowded.

Questions 5 and 6 refer to the following passage about economic competition.

In economics, competition refers to the interaction between buyers and sellers as they establish prices and exchange goods and services. According to theory, economic competition serves the needs of both individuals and society. When buyers compete with buyers and sellers compete with sellers, the maximum amount of goods is produced at the best possible price.

The theory of competition is based on the assumption that rivalry in the marketplace keeps things in balance. Producers must use their resources in ways that best satisfy consumers. Thus, a business that sells a similar product at a higher price than other businesses will not find buyers. A job seeker who asks more than the usual wage will not get the job. An employer who pays less than competing employers will not find competent workers.

5. Which of the following is an opinion about competition based on the passage?

   (1) Competition is an important part of the U.S. economic system.
   (2) The main goal of competition is to keep prices down.
   (3) Competition works better than any other economic system.
   (4) Intense competition for jobs helps keep wages down.
   (5) Competition assures the maximum number of goods will be produced at any price.

6. Based on the passage, which of the following is a fact about competition?

   (1) Automobile manufacturers compete with each other for the consumer's business.
   (2) An expensive car cannot be sold in a competitive system.
   (3) A retail salesperson cannot ask for a raise in a competitive market.
   (4) The worker who will accept the lowest wage is most likely to get the job.
   (5) Competition pushes car prices up to make them more attractive.

Question 7 refers to the following charts.

Chicago-Area Construction Firms: Ownership and Earnings

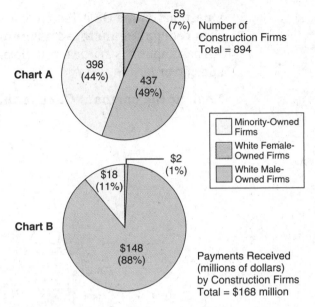

Chart A

398 (44%)
437 (49%)
59 (7%)

Number of Construction Firms Total = 894

Minority-Owned Firms
White Female-Owned Firms
White Male-Owned Firms

Chart B

$18 (11%)
$2 (1%)
$148 (88%)

Payments Received (millions of dollars) by Construction Firms Total = $168 million

7. Which of the following is an opinion based on the information in the chart?

   (1) Firms owned by white males received the highest percentage of the total paid for construction services.
   (2) Firms owned by white females received the lowest percentage of the total paid for construction services.
   (3) Together, firms owned by white females and minorities received a little over 10% of the total paid for construction services.
   (4) Together, firms owned by white females and minorities were paid about $20 million for construction services.
   (5) White males have nothing to complain about when it comes to their role in the construction business.

> **TIP**
>
> **Words that indicate judgment or emotion are signals of opinions. Watch for words such as _talented_, _dull_, _good_, and _bad_.**

Answers and explanations start on page 112.

Recognize Unstated Assumptions

Questions on the GED Test may ask you to read a passage or look at a graphic and then **recognize unstated assumptions** on which the passage or graphic is based. An assumption is an idea, principle, or theory we take for granted or believe without specific proof.

Look at the cartoon. Choose the <u>one best answer</u> to the question.

QUESTION: What does the cartoonist assume the audience already knows?

(1) China wants to control Taiwan.
(2) Lions are still a popular Asian symbol.
(3) Taiwan is a weak and defenseless country.
(4) The Great Wall of China is an obstacle between China and Taiwan.
(5) Taiwan is currently a part of the People's Republic of China.

EXPLANATIONS

STEP 1

To answer this question, ask yourself:

- What is this cartoon about? <u>A huge lion, which represents China, is roping the smaller Taiwan.</u>
- What is the question asking me to do? <u>Recognize the logical assumptions on which the cartoon is based.</u>

STEP 2

Evaluate all the answer choices and choose the <u>best</u> answer.

(1) Yes. China has always felt that Taiwan belonged to the mainland. This idea is represented by the lion pulling Taiwan closer to China.
(2) No. This option is true but irrelevant to the cartoon.
(3) No. Taiwan's small size in the cartoon does not mean it is weak and defenseless.
(4) No. This option is false.
(5) No. This option is incorrect and contradicts the cartoon.

ANSWER: (1) China wants to control Taiwan.

Practice the Skill

Try these examples. Choose the <u>one best answer</u> to each question. Then check your answers and the explanations.

In July 1863, Confederate and Union forces met on the battlefield in Gettysburg, Pennsylvania. They fought for three days, and the two sides suffered more than 45,000 casualties. In 1863, the battlefield at Gettysburg was established as a national cemetery to honor the Union dead. It became a national military park in 1895. At the cemetery's dedication in November 1863, President Lincoln spoke for only two minutes, but his eloquent speech is one of the most famous in U.S. history. Here is the first sentence of the speech: *Four score and seven years ago our fathers brought forth on this continent a new nation, conceived in liberty, and dedicated to the proposition that all men are created equal.*

1. Which of the following may have been a basic assumption behind the decision to establish a national cemetery at Gettysburg?

   (1) The site should be designated as a final resting place for Union soldiers killed.
   (2) The Gettysburg cemetery lands would become a national military park in 1895.
   (3) The idea of a national military park and the visitors it might draw held appeal to local businesses.
   (4) As a Southern state, Pennsylvania wanted to honor the Confederate dead at Gettysburg.
   (5) The cemetery would honor all those who died there.

   HINT Why would local authorities have made an effort to seek designation for a national cemetery at Gettysburg?

2. During his Gettysburg speech, Lincoln assumed his audience knew that the first sentence was a reference to

   (1) the War of 1812, fought by the generation immediately before Lincoln's
   (2) the signers of the Pennsylvania Constitution
   (3) the French and Indian Wars
   (4) Lincoln's own eloquence
   (5) the people behind the creation of the Declaration of Independence in 1776

   HINT What information does the first sentence of the Gettysburg Address assume Lincoln's audience already knew?

Answers and Explanations

1. (1) The site should be designated as a final resting place for Union soldiers killed.
Option (1) correctly identifies the central assumption that came before the decision to create the national cemetery in 1863.

Options (2) and (3) are incorrect because no one could have known that the lands would become a national military park in 1895, more than 30 years later, and the original purpose for the cemetery was to honor the Union dead. Options (4) and (5) are incorrect because Pennsylvania was a Northern state during the war; its soldiers were Union soldiers, and the cemetery would be to honor the Union dead at Gettysburg.

2. (5) the people behind the creation of the Declaration of Independence in 1776
Option (5) correctly identifies the assumptions Lincoln makes in the first sentence of his address.

Options (1), (2), and (3) are incorrect because the phrase does not refer to the War of 1812, the signers of the Pennsylvania Constitution, or the French and Indian Wars. Although Lincoln's speech was eloquent (option 4), this is not what the sentence is referencing.

Recognize Unstated Assumptions

Directions: Choose the <u>one best answer</u> to each question.

<u>Questions 1 and 2</u> refer to the following graph about employment-based health insurance.

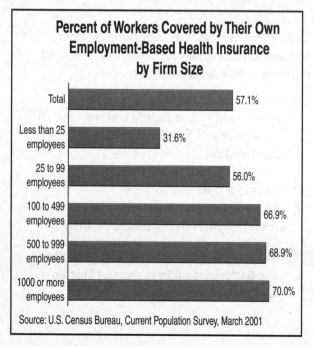

Percent of Workers Covered by Their Own Employment-Based Health Insurance by Firm Size

Total — 57.1%
Less than 25 employees — 31.6%
25 to 99 employees — 56.0%
100 to 499 employees — 66.9%
500 to 999 employees — 68.9%
1000 or more employees — 70.0%

Source: U.S. Census Bureau, Current Population Survey, March 2001

1. Which of the following statements is implied by the information in the graph?

   (1) The majority of Americans work for big companies.
   (2) Americans are not concerned about insurance.
   (3) Not all employers provide insurance to their workers.
   (4) Most Americans do not have health coverage.
   (5) The only way to get health insurance is through your employer.

2. Based on the graph, which of the following is an unstated assumption about companies with fewer than 25 employees?

   (1) They are paid less than employees at companies of any other size.
   (2) They are less likely to offer insurance.
   (3) They offer mostly low-skill jobs.
   (4) They are not very profitable.
   (5) They do not care about employees.

<u>Question 3</u> refers to this passage about environment and population.

The number of people who live in an area is related to the number of the resources available in that area. Many of Earth's coastal regions are heavily populated, in part because of the readily available supply of fish. On the other hand, the polar regions of North America and Asia are home to relatively few people. Although plenty of water and game are available, the absence of trees deprives residents of wood for shelter and fuel.

3. Which of the following is an unstated assumption from the paragraph?

   (1) Most people who live on Earth's coasts earn their living by fishing.
   (2) Coastal regions tend to have mild climates, so people want to live there.
   (3) Fish are a major source of food for many of the world's people.
   (4) There are no trees in the coastal regions.
   (5) Many of the world's polar regions are rich in oil resources.

> **TIP**
>
> Assumptions are almost always unstated. Watch for ideas or images that are not explained. Political cartoons, especially, rely on symbols, images, and special wording that the cartoonist assumes the reader understands.

Questions 4 through 6 refer to the following passage about credit files.

A credit bureau is an organization that businesses contact when they want credit information on prospective customers. Under the U.S. Fair Credit Reporting Act, all individuals can inspect their credit files by contacting a credit bureau. These bureaus are listed in the telephone book under "Credit Rating" or "Reporting Agencies." If an individual is denied credit because of negative information reported by a credit bureau, that person has a right to review his or her credit files within 30 days of the denial at no charge.

After inspecting this record of past credit behavior, a consumer can challenge any item that appears questionable or inaccurate. The credit bureau must then investigate and remove any item it cannot substantiate. If the credit bureau deletes an unsubstantiated item from the file, the consumer may ask the credit bureau to inform any party who received a report within the past six months.

4. Which of the following situations would most likely cause individuals to review their credit?

(1) an overcharge on a credit card bill
(2) a denial of credit
(3) a late fee on a credit card bill
(4) the receipt of a new credit card
(5) an application for a new credit card

5. What basic assumption underlies the Fair Credit Reporting Act?

(1) A good, accurate credit rating carries great importance.
(2) The use of consumer credit is excessive.
(3) Consumers need to save more and spend less.
(4) Consumers cannot trust lenders.
(5) Consumers are entitled to privacy in their business dealings.

6. Which of the following assumptions can you make about the Fair Credit Reporting Act?

(1) It interferes with the rights of consumers.
(2) It is designed to protect credit bureaus.
(3) It is designed to protect consumers.
(4) It promotes the excessive use of credit.
(5) It discourages the use of credit.

Question 7 refers to the following table and passage about racism in South Africa.

South Africa During Apartheid		
	Whites	*Blacks*
Population	4.5 million	19 million
Land ownership	87 percent	13 percent
National income	75 percent	< 20 percent
Doctor/population	1/400	1/44,000
Infant mortality rate	2.7%	30%
Yearly per pupil expenditure	$696	$45
Teacher/pupil	1/22	1/60

Until the recent abolition of apartheid, racism against black and mixed-descent Africans was practiced openly in South Africa. The Population Registration Act of 1950 required all South Africans to register as black, white, or colored. Classification was determined by physical appearance. Among other restrictions, apartheid laws forbade marriage of nonwhites to whites, protected white-only jobs, and barred non-whites from entering white-only neighborhoods.

7. The lives of black citizens in South Africa during apartheid were most likely

(1) hopeful and upwardly-mobile
(2) impoverished and oppressed
(3) long-lived and rewarding
(4) equal to those of white Africans
(5) better than the lives of black citizens in other African nations

Answers and explanations start on page 113.

Skill 8

Identify Causes and Effects

Some questions on the GED Test will ask you to **identify causes** and **effects** presented in a passage or graphic. A cause is what makes something happen, while an effect is the result of a cause. For example, you might get a speeding ticket. The cause was the fact that you were speeding. The effect might be that you'll drive slower in the future.

Read the passage. Choose the <u>one best answer</u> to the question.

Foreign policy in the United States changes frequently because it is controlled by the current president. Each president approaches foreign policy differently. Also, because the members of the Cabinet change with the administration, the advice given to each president varies. Most presidents are remembered for one special foreign policy. Richard Nixon's policy of détente (easing tensions between nations) resulted in better relations with China. Jimmy Carter helped create a peace treaty between Israel and Egypt. Ronald Reagan focused on anticommunism. George Bush aimed for a "new world order." Bill Clinton tried to improve relations between Palestine and Israel. George W. Bush tried to erase world terrorism.

QUESTION: According to the passage, variation in U.S. foreign policy is a result of which of the following?

(1) presidents changing their minds
(2) cabinets giving confusing advice
(3) the rest of the world changing
(4) presidents making their own foreign policy
(5) presidents lacking foreign policy background

EXPLANATIONS

STEP 1 To answer this question, ask yourself:

- What is this passage about? <u>variations in presidential foreign policy</u>
- What is the question asking me to do? <u>Identify the cause of the variations.</u>

STEP 2 Evaluate all the answer choices and choose the best answer.

(1) No. This is not addressed in the passage.
(2) No. Advice from the Cabinet is described as varying, not confusing.
(3) No. While U.S. policy is affected by world changes, it is made by the president.
(4) Yes. Because each president takes a different approach, U.S. foreign policy varies.
(5) No. This is not addressed in the passage.

ANSWER: **(4) presidents making their own foreign policy**

Practice the Skill

Try these examples. Choose the one best answer to each question. Then check your answers and the explanations.

Early attempts to form strong national unions were short-lived. The Knights of Labor formed in 1869 but lost its power after the violent Haymarket Riot in 1886.

The American Federation of Labor (AFL), first called Federation of Organized Trades and Labor Unions (FOTLU), came into being in 1881. The AFL was unlike other unions in several ways. Its goals were economic instead of political. It also limited its action to helping skilled workers instead of trying to help all laborers. The AFL was the first successful collection of small craft unions.

American Federation of Labor Total Union Membership	
1910	2,116,000
1909	1,965,000
1908	2,092,000
1907	2,077,000
1906	1,892,000
1905	1,918,000
1904	2,067,000
1903	1,824,000
1902	1,335,000
1901	1,058,000
1900	791,000
1899	550,000
1898	467,000
1897	440,000

1. Based on the information from the table and the passage, what was an effect of the AFL's success?

   (1) an overall rise in membership
   (2) a decrease in membership
   (3) the breakup of the AFL in 1910
   (4) an increase in skilled workers
   (5) a decrease in unskilled union members.

   HINT Which statement can you verify from the table?

2. According to the passage, the AFL's success was the result of which of the following?

   (1) the failure of the Knights of Labor
   (2) its practical goals
   (3) the long history of craft unions
   (4) the Industrial Revolution
   (5) its political agenda

   HINT Why was the AFL successful?

Answers and Explanations

1. (1) an overall rise in membership
Option (1) is correct, as indicated by the overall increase in membership numbers after 1897.

Option (2) is directly contradicted by information in the table. Option (3) is incorrect; while the table provides membership data only through 1910, there is no suggestion that the AFL broke up in 1910. Option (4) is incorrect because there is no information regarding an increase in skilled workers. The passage does not support a decrease in unskilled union members (option 5).

2. (2) its practical goals
Option (2) is correct because the passage states that the AFL's goals were economic rather than political and were more focused and specifc than those of previous unions.

The rise of the AFL was not dependent upon the demise of the Knights of Labor (option 1). Options (3) and (4) are not causes of the union's success. Option (5) is incorrect because the passage states that the AFL had an economic agenda.

Identify Causes and Effects

Directions: Choose the one best answer to each question.

Questions 1 and 2 refer to the following passage about global warming.

Carbon dioxide, or CO_2, is a gas in the atmosphere that regulates Earth's temperature. Over time, however, human activity, like burning fossil fuels such as coal, oil, and gas, has doubled the levels of CO_2 in the atmosphere. The cutting and burning of forests also raises CO_2 levels. Trees soak up CO_2 when alive. Many scientists agree that these activities are causing a gradual warming of the planet.

Global warming could have many severe consequences. As the polar ice caps melt, sea levels could rise, flooding coastal areas and leaving millions homeless. As temperatures rise, food harvests could decline drastically.

1. According to the passage, global warming is caused by

   (1) rising sea levels and declining food harvests
   (2) melting polar ice caps
   (3) declining CO_2 gas levels
   (4) the burning of fossil fuels and destruction of forests
   (5) thawing of northern regions and changes in the atmosphere

2. Which cause-and-effect statement is accurate based on the passage?

   (1) Global warming could decrease the land area where people can live.
   (2) Global warming could cause CO_2 levels to rise.
   (3) Rising CO_2 levels destroy forests.
   (4) Increased CO_2 levels are a result of global warming.
   (5) Coastal flooding will decrease the marine life population.

Questions 3 and 4 refer to the following photograph and passage.

When Charles Lindbergh flew the *Spirit of St. Louis,* a small monoplane, from Long Island to Paris, he became the first person to fly nonstop across the Atlantic Ocean. Lindbergh's flight fascinated millions of people and made commercial air travel seem possible.

3. What was a lasting result of Lindbergh's flight?

   (1) The plane now hangs in a museum.
   (2) He improved relations with France.
   (3) Commercial air travel became a popular form of transportation.
   (4) Long Island became an important transportation hub.
   (5) Many people wanted to become pilots.

4. Which effect of Lindbergh's feat does the photograph depict?

   (1) People like to gather in large crowds.
   (2) The public became fascinated with airplanes.
   (3) Charles Lindbergh became a recluse.
   (4) People were bored by the *Spirit of St. Louis.*
   (5) Many cities built new airports.

Questions 5 and 6 refer to the following passage.

The term *supply-side economics* refers to the belief that economic growth will result if the government lowers taxes. Specifically, the theory holds that if taxes are reduced, consumers and businesses will have more money to spend, save, and invest. In turn, business will expand, as will production and employment. Furthermore, the theory states that tax cuts will not reduce the government's tax revenues because increased prosperity will offset the effects of lower tax rates.

This philosophy fueled the Reagan tax cuts of the 1980s. Supply-side supporters maintained that the tax cuts spurred economic growth. Critics argued that the cuts produced a massive federal deficit and unfairly penalized the poor and middle class.

5. According to the passage, what effect does a high tax rate have on the economy?

   (1) It creates jobs for the poor.
   (2) It leads to economic growth.
   (3) It leads to inflation.
   (4) It slows down the economy.
   (5) It allows the government to invest in business.

6. Based on the passage, which of the following might a critic of supply-side economics cite as a potential result of tax cuts?

   (1) a reduction in funds for food stamps and Medicaid
   (2) a decrease in manufactured goods
   (3) an increase in housing construction
   (4) a decrease in investment in technological research
   (5) a decline in sales to foreign countries

Questions 7 and 8 refer to the following pie chart about Earth's surface.

Composition of Earth's Surface

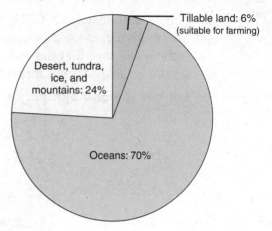

7. Which statement best summarizes the information in the chart?

   (1) Most of Earth's surface does not support human life.
   (2) Tillable land makes up almost half of the land on Earth's surface.
   (3) Most of Earth's surface is water while less than one-third of the surface is land.
   (4) The oceans are expanding and will soon cover a greater portion of the land.
   (5) Earth is equally divided between land and water.

8. Based on the chart, what might be one effect of population growth on Earth?

   (1) increased demand on the tillable land
   (2) decreased rate of global warming
   (3) decreased percentage of tillable land
   (4) increased percentage of desert land
   (5) decreased water pollution

[**TIP**]

To identify a cause-and-effect relationship, look for something that makes another thing happen. Some key words that show cause and effect are: *as a result, therefore, since, because, due to this, thus,* and *so.*

Answers and explanations start on page 113.

Evaluation

Draw Conclusions

Some questions on the GED Social Studies Test will ask you to **draw conclusions** from information presented in a passage or graphic. A conclusion is a logical idea based on facts. Make sure that the conclusions you draw are based on evidence in the text. You should be able to use information from the text to explain the conclusions that you draw.

Look at the photograph. Choose the <u>one best answer</u> to the question.

QUESTION: The woman in the photograph is celebrating her birthday. What can you conclude about her culture?

In this woman's culture

    (1) the elderly are not respected
    (2) most grandmothers live with their children
    (3) special foods play a role in celebrations
    (4) everybody celebrates birthdays
    (5) men don't celebrate birthdays

EXPLANATIONS

STEP 1

To answer this question, ask yourself:

- What does the photograph show? <u>a woman being presented with a cake</u>
- What is the question asking me to do? <u>Apply the information communicated by the photograph to draw a specific conclusion.</u>

STEP 2

Evaluate all the answer choices and choose the best answer.

    (1) No. This cannot be concluded from the photograph and contradicts the visual message of the occasion.
    (2) No. While some grandmothers may live with their children, nothing in the photograph suggests most do.
    (3) Yes. Special foods, such as cakes, are an important part of parties.
    (4) No. There is no information in the photograph that suggests all members of the woman's culture celebrate birthdays, although this may be true.
    (5) No. While the photograph does not include men, you cannot conclude they do not celebrate birthdays.

ANSWER: (3) special foods play a role in celebrations

Practice the Skill

Try these examples. Choose the **one best answer** to each question. Then check your answers and the explanations.

Massachusetts Voting Districts, 2001

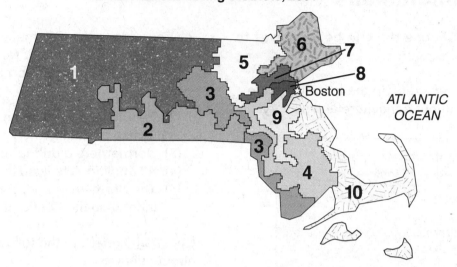

1. Knowing that each district has the same number of people, which of the following can you conclude from the map?

    (1) Districts 7, 8, and 9 are the wealthiest.
    (2) Boston is located in district 5.
    (3) Most people are Democrats.
    (4) Western Massachusetts is not heavily populated.
    (5) Most people in Massachusetts vote.

    HINT If each district has the same number of people, what would it mean if a district were very large?

2. Why might the map need to be redrawn after the federal census?

    (1) Districts are automatically redrawn every ten years.
    (2) More polling places are needed after the census.
    (3) The population gets older.
    (4) Massachusetts residents change their political allegiances.
    (5) People move into and out of districts.

    HINT A census is a survey which could determine the number of people in a district.

Answers and Explanations

1. (4) Western Massachusetts is not heavily populated.

Option (4) is correct. District 1, in western Massachusetts, is spread over the largest geographic area, indicating its population is the least concentrated, making it the least heavily populated.

The map does not give information about wealth (option 1), political party (option 3), or voting habits (option 5). Option (2) is contradicted by the map, which locates Boston in the area of districts 8 and 9.

2. (5) People move into and out of districts.

Option (5) is correct: a new census might identify changing population numbers in districts. To maintain the same number of people in each district, this may require district boundaries to be redrawn.

The map does not give information about automatic adjustments to the district boundaries (option 1), polling places (option 2), population age (option 3), or voters' political party loyalties (option 4).

Draw Conclusions

Directions: Choose the <u>one best answer</u> to each question.

<u>Questions 1 and 2</u> refer to the following table and passage about agriculture and slavery.

Agricultural Production, 1860
<u>North</u>
New York . . . . dairy
Massachusetts . . . . alfalfa
Pennsylvania . . . . wheat
<u>South</u>
Georgia . . . . cotton
North Carolina . . . . tobacco

Initially, Southerners regarded slavery as a "necessary evil." However, after the invention of the cotton gin in 1793, cotton became the primary crop of Southern states. The cotton plantation economy depended heavily on slave labor. As the industry grew, Southerners began to defend slavery as actually good for the slaves.

At first, Northerners were indifferent to the slavery issue. Eventually, the protests of abolitionists made a difference. They urged people to take a moral stand against the ownership of human beings. The anti-slavery movement soon took hold in the Northern states.

1. Based on the information in the passage, which of the following can you conclude?

   (1) The cotton gin helped end slavery.
   (2) Americans never approved of slavery.
   (3) Economic issues influenced Southerners' attitudes toward slavery.
   (4) Southerners were not interested in moral issues.
   (5) Southerners treated their slaves well.

2. According to the information in the table and the passage, why might Northerners have been less likely to support slavery?

   (1) Northerners were more humane people.
   (2) People who lived in the North were British citizens.
   (3) Northerners didn't farm.
   (4) All abolitionists lived in the North.
   (5) The Northern economy relied less on slave labor than the Southern economy did.

<u>Question 3</u> refers to the following passage about culture.

The term "culture" refers to the beliefs, attitudes, values, customs, and ideals of a society or population. Using money to purchase goods, wearing certain clothes to a wedding, or eating certain foods are all part of a society's culture. The world has many cultures, and the customs of each one differ dramatically. For example, many North Americans enjoy eating beef. In contrast, Hindus in India consider the cow to be a sacred animal, and eating beef would be sacrilegious. Our attitudes about eating beef are established by the customs of our culture.

3. Based on the passage, what can you conclude about food preferences?

   (1) No matter what culture you live in, eating beef is not considered disgusting.
   (2) Food preferences are often determined by cultural influences.
   (3) A Hindu living in North America could probably learn to like eating beef.
   (4) Beef could become an Indian delicacy.
   (5) Eating beef is wrong.

Questions 4 and 5 refer to the following photograph and passage about the Civil War.

Union forces adopted a new strategy for war in 1864. General Sherman wrote, "We are not only fighting hostile armies, but a hostile people." On his march through Georgia and South Carolina in 1864 and 1865, General Sherman practiced what became known as "total war."

Union soldiers destroyed fields, factories, homes, railroads, and anything else that might support the Confederate army. The total ruin of the Southern infrastructure brought about the collapse of Confederate forces and complete victory for the North.

4. Which of the following can you conclude from the photograph and passage?

   (1) Southern war strategy did not include the defense of its cities.
   (2) Union forces were unsuccessful against the Confederate army.
   (3) Southern cities were utterly devastated by the war.
   (4) The concept of total war applied only to the Confederate army.
   (5) Union war strategy distinguished between civilian and military targets.

5. From the information on the Civil War, it can be concluded that General Sherman

   (1) pursued only military targets
   (2) believed "total war" was necessary for victory
   (3) hated all Southerners
   (4) cared about the effect of war on civilians
   (5) followed accepted rules of warfare

Questions 6 and 7 refer to the following passage about voting.

The majority of Americans who are eligible to vote do not. One study of voter turnout recorded a direct correlation between income level and voter participation. The report showed that 80 percent of eligible voters who made $50,000 and over a year voted, while only 52 percent of eligible voters making between $10,000 and $20,000 chose to vote.

6. Based on the information in the passage, which of the following groups or locations is likely to have the highest voter turnout?

   (1) a low-income neighborhood
   (2) a college political science class
   (3) retired people
   (4) women
   (5) a wealthy suburb

7. Based on the passage, if a vote were taken in a district containing all income levels, which of the following would be most likely to pass?

   (1) an income tax break
   (2) an increase in property taxes
   (3) a subsidized school lunch program
   (4) expanded welfare benefits
   (5) a low-income tax credit

> **TIP**
>
> Any conclusion you draw must take into account all the evidence that is given in a passage or graphic.

Answers and explanations start on page 114.

Skill 10

Evaluate Support for Generalizations

Questions on the GED Social Studies Test may ask you to **evaluate** the **support** provided in a passage or graphic for **generalizations** made about the information. Providing evidence for a generalization is important. You must be able to evaluate the information provided and make a generalization, or broad statement, that is fully supported by the text or graphic.

Read the passage below. Choose the <u>one best answer</u> to the question.

Industrialization develops as societies replace human and animal muscle power with advanced sources of energy. Formally, an industrial society is one that produces goods using sophisticated machinery powered by fossil fuels and nuclear energy. Industrial technology has raised living standards and extended life for millions of people.

"First world" refers to industrial societies based on capitalism. The "second world" is composed of the current and former communist nations, most of which are currently transforming their socialist economies into market-driven systems. The "third world" refers to underdeveloped or developing countries where living standards are low.

QUESTION: Which of the following generalizations is supported by the passage?

(1) Economists agree that first-world nations are the most important.
(2) The standard of living in third-world nations is approaching first-world status.
(3) The United States and Europe could be considered part of the third world.
(4) Poverty only exists in second- and third-world nations.
(5) Nations can be classified based on technological and economic development.

EXPLANATIONS

STEP 1

To answer this question, ask yourself:

• What is the passage about? <u>industrialization and the division of the world into developed and developing countries</u>
• What is the question asking me to do? <u>Identify the generalization that is supported by statements in the passage.</u>

STEP 2

Evaluate all the answer choices and choose the <u>best</u> answer.

(1) No. The passage does not suggest that economists think first-world nations are most important.
(2) No. The passage states that living standards in the third world are low and does not suggest that they are rising to those of the first world.
(3) No. The passage neither states nor suggests that the U.S. and Europe could be considered part of the third world.
(4) No. The passage does not suggest that no one in first-world countries lives in poverty.
(5) Yes. The descriptions of first, second, and third world nations support the generalization that nations can be classified by technological and economic development.

ANSWER: (5) Nations can be classified based on technological and economic development.

Practice the Skill

Try these examples. Choose the <u>one best answer</u> to each question. Then check your answers and the explanations.

The U.S. economy of today is often referred to as "postindustrial." Postindustrial economies focus on the production of services and information, not manufactured goods. This term reflects the trends that occurred during the twentieth century in the three main sectors of the workforce: the farming sector; the blue-collar sector (manufacturing and construction); and the white-collar, or service, sector. White-collar work includes occupations from doctors and lawyers to salesclerks and secretaries.

Work Patterns in the United States, 1900–2000

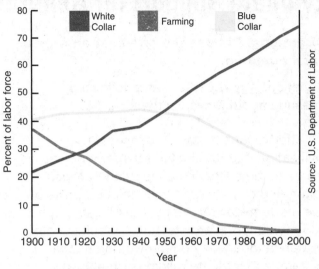

Source: U.S. Department of Labor

1. Which of the following generalizations is supported by the graph?

   (1) A service economy is on the rise while manufacturing is on the decline.
   (2) U.S. blue-collar labor has grown steadily over the past century.
   (3) Government support to U.S. farmers has decreased since the 1930s.
   (4) Earnings for white-collar workers have increased steadily since 1900.
   (5) Farm workers are now competing with blue-collar workers for jobs.

   HINT Which idea is best supported by the graph?

2. Which trend <u>best</u> supports the generalization that the United States has a postindustrial economy?

   (1) decline in the farming sector
   (2) increase in the white-collar sector
   (3) increase in the white-collar sector plus decrease in the blue-collar sector
   (4) decrease in the farming sector plus decrease in the blue-collar sector
   (5) the large gap between the farming and white-collar sectors

   HINT Which trend shows a focus on the production of services and information, not manufactured goods?

Answers and Explanations

1. (1) A service economy is on the rise while manufacturing is on the decline.
Option (1) is correct because, as the graph shows, the white-collar portion of the labor force grew steadily to about 70 percent in 2000 while the blue-collar force had declined to about 25 percent by that date.

Option (2) is incorrect because the graph shows the blue-collar force is on the decline. Options (3), (4), and (5) are incorrect because the graph does not address government support to farmers, earnings for white-collar workers, or competition between farmers and blue-collar workers for jobs.

2. (3) increase in the white-collar sector plus decrease in the blue-collar sector
Option (3) is correct. These changes show a decrease in manufacturing and an increase in the service sector.

Options (1), (4), and (5) are incorrect because postindustrialism is not defined by the farming sector. Option (2) is incorrect because an increase in the white-collar sector is only part of the trend.

Evaluate Support for Generalizations

Directions: Choose the one best answer to each question.

Questions 1 and 2 refer to the following passage about Mayan culture.

The Mayans created a successful civilization that dominated Mesoamerica at the same time Charlemagne ruled Europe. Extending over an area that included parts of five modern-day countries, the Mayan empire had monumental architecture, a sophisticated written language, a complex mathematical system, and intricate religious rituals.

Much of what we know about Mayan culture has come from reading Mayan glyphs, their system of writing with pictures and symbols. The glyphs were not understood very well until recently. Unfortunately, a Spanish bishop destroyed all but four known Mayan books in the 1500s. However, breakthroughs were made in the 1960s. Now researchers realize the glyphs combine syllables, symbols, emblems, and ideas to form a phonetic system.

1. Which of the following generalizations is supported by the fact that most Mayan books were destroyed?

   (1) The bishop spared the four best books.
   (2) The Mayan system of writing included phonetics.
   (3) Scholars did not try to understand the glyphs until recently.
   (4) Deciphering Mayan glyphs was difficult with so few resources available.
   (5) Mayan glyphs are extremely complicated.

> **TIP**
>
> When you look for supporting statements, look for facts, figures, details, and examples that back up an idea, or generalization.

2. Which of the following details best supports the generalization that Mayan civilization was intellectually advanced?

   (1) The Mayan empire included parts of five modern-day countries.
   (2) The Mayans were able to defeat the Spaniards.
   (3) The Mayans ruled at the same time as Charlemagne.
   (4) The Mayans were a religious people.
   (5) The Mayans developed a complex mathematical system.

Question 3 refers to the following photograph of an Egyptian wall painting.

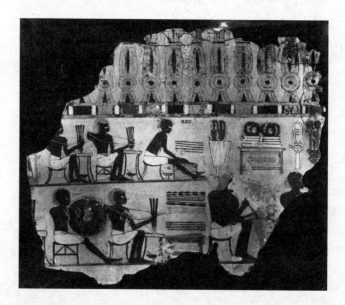

3. This painting from the tomb of Sebekhotep, a senior treasury official in ancient Egypt, depicts artisans at work making jewelry. Which of the following generalizations is supported by the information in the painting?

   (1) Early Egyptians were a skilled, industrious people.
   (2) All Egyptians owned jewelry.
   (3) Sebekhotep was a painter.
   (4) Egyptians had stockpiles of gold.
   (5) All Egyptian tombs contained artwork.

Question 4 refers to the following passage about artificial life support.

"Artificial life support" refers to medical technology that aids, supports, or replaces vital functions of the body that have been damaged or destroyed. The use of these systems to prolong a patient's life raises such ethical issues as the quality of life and the right to die.

It also raises economic issues, since the cost of providing artificial life support can be enormous. In the United States, most medical care is financed by private coverage and government programs. These insurers place limits on the costs they will cover.

4. Which of the following generalizations is best supported by the passage?

(1) The development of artificial life support systems has no economic implications.
(2) The economic issues surrounding artificial life support have more impact than the ethical issues.
(3) New technology and economic issues affect each other in complex ways.
(4) Most people want artificial life support despite the ethical dilemmas.
(5) People are entitled to artificial life support despite the cost.

Question 5 refers to the following passage about the Code of Hammurabi.

Hammurabi ruled Babylon around 1800 B.C. His legal code, believed to be the first formal set of laws ever created, was found over 100 years ago on a stone slab in Iran. The concept of severe punishment, often called "an eye for an eye," was the basis for many of the approximately 282 laws that make up the Code.

5. Which of the following generalizations is best supported by the passage?

(1) Hammurabi was a ruthless leader.
(2) Hammurabi advocated harsh penalties for crimes.
(3) The slab found in Iran is a hoax.
(4) Babylonians were especially violent.
(5) Many of Hammurabi's laws are still used.

Questions 6 and 7 refer to the following cartoon.

6. Which of the following generalizations does the cartoon support?

(1) Traffic problems have increased enormously over the past 15 years.
(2) People prefer living in cities.
(3) People think cities are more important than rain forests.
(4) Destruction of rain forests has occurred at a surprisingly rapid pace.
(5) People are suffering because the rain forests have been destroyed.

7. According to the cartoon, what generalization can be made about urban development?

(1) It has raised the standard of living for native peoples.
(2) It has preserved the natural environment wherever possible.
(3) It has provided much-needed jobs for people.
(4) It has made Earth more beautiful.
(5) It has damaged Earth's natural habitats.

Answers and explanations start on page 114.

Skill 11

Tables and Charts

Some questions on the GED Social Studies Test will ask you to read **tables** or **charts**. Tables and charts organize information in rows and columns. For example, you could look at a table or chart and then be asked to identify its implications, to describe causes and effects, to draw conclusions, to recognize or restate a main idea, or to summarize information, as in the question below.

Study the table. Choose the <u>one best answer</u> to the question.

What Cass County pays to the U.S. Government	In millions
Income taxes	$186
Payroll taxes	160
Corporate and excise taxes	60
TOTAL	$406
What Cass County Gets Back	
Direct payments to individuals	$226
Salaries	97
Grant awards	72
Other expenditures	102
Procurements	19
Direct loans	14
TOTAL	$530
Cass County's Net Benefit	($124)

Source: North Dakota Census Data Center

QUESTION:

Which of the following <u>best</u> summarizes Cass County's relationship with the federal government?

(1) Cass County pays little federal corporate tax.
(2) Cass County has many federal employees.
(3) Cass County residents pay federal taxes.
(4) Cass County receives more federal funding than it pays.
(5) Cass County receives federal grants.

EXPLANATIONS

STEP 1 To answer this question, ask yourself:

- What information is displayed in the table? <u>Cass County money paid to and received from the federal government and Cass County's net benefit</u>
- What is the question asking me to do? <u>Identify the statement that best summarizes the main points of the table.</u>

STEP 2 Evaluate all of the answer choices and choose the <u>best</u> answer.

(1) No. The table does not compare Cass County's tax liability to other counties.
(2) No. The table does not indicate the number of federal employees.
(3) No. Whether or not Cass County's residents pay federal taxes is not the table's main idea.
(4) **Yes. This option summarizes the table's three labels: the amount Cass County pays, the amount it gets back, and its net benefit.**
(5) No. Federal grant income is a detail, not the main point.

ANSWER: (4) Cass County receives more federal funding than it pays.

Practice the Skill

Try these examples. Choose the <u>one best answer</u> to each question. Then check your answers and read the explanations.

The Thirteen Original Colonies

COLONY NAME	YEAR FOUNDED	FOUNDED BY	BECAME ROYAL COLONY
Virginia	1607	London Company	1624
Massachusetts	1620	Puritans	1691
New Hampshire	1623	John Wheelwright	1679
Maryland	1634	Lord Baltimore	1634
Connecticut	c. 1635	Thomas Hooker	1635
Rhode Island	1636	Roger Williams	1644
Delaware	1638	Peter Minuit and New Sweden Company	1691
North Carolina	1653	Virginians	1729
South Carolina	1663	Eight nobles with a Royal Charter from Charles II	1729
New Jersey	1664	Lord Berkeley and Sir George Carteret	1702
New York	1664	Duke of York	1685
Pennsylvania	1682	William Penn	1682
Georgia	1732	James Edward Oglethorpe	1752

1. Which of the following restates information about Maryland, Connecticut, and Delaware?

(1) They were founded within a four-year period.
(2) They were not originally royal colonies.
(3) They were originally part of Virginia.
(4) They formed the Middle Atlantic colonies.
(5) They were founded by the Puritans.

HINT What information is in the chart?

2. Which of the following conclusions can be drawn from the chart?

(1) The Southern colonies were founded before those in the Middle Atlantic and New England regions.
(2) By 1752, all 13 colonies were under royal control.
(3) The Duke of York was the first colonial governor of New York.
(4) Life under British control was difficult.
(5) It was easy to found a colony.

HINT What logical conclusion do the facts of the chart allow you to reach?

Answers and Explanations

1. (1) They were founded within a four-year period.

Option (1) restates the information from the chart indicating these three colonies were founded within the period beginning in 1634 (Maryland) and ending in 1638 (Delaware).

Option (2) is incorrect; the chart shows that Maryland and Connecticut were originally royal colonies. Options (3) and (4) are incorrect and not supported by the chart. Option (5) is incorrect and contradicted by the chart, which shows that Massachusetts was the only colony founded by the Puritans.

2. (2) By 1752, all 13 colonies were under royal control.

Option (2) is correct; you can see from the last column that all colonies were under royal control by 1752.

The chart does not indicate that Southern colonies were founded before the Middle Atlantic and New England colonies (option 1). Nothing in the chart supports consideration that the Duke of York was New York's first colonial governor (option 3). The facts of the chart don't address the ease or difficulty of life (option 4). Option (5) is incorrect and not supported by the facts in the chart.

Tables and Charts

Directions: Choose the **one best answer** to each question.

Questions 1 through 4 refer to the following table.

State Budget Cuts and Additions	
Public Schools	− $250.3 million
Criminal Justice Systems	− $125.2 million
Community Colleges	− $ 30.8 million
State University System	− $ 78.2 million
Transportation	− $ 29.2 million
Scholarships	− $ 8.1 million
Substance Abuse Treatment Program	− $ 3.4 million
Welfare-to-Work Training	+ $ 8.9 million
Tourism Promotion	+ $ 27.2 million
Highway Construction	+ $328.1 million
School Construction	+ $223.1 million
Security	+ $ 28.7 million
Tax Incentives	+ $428.3 million

1. Which of the following best restates the information in the table?

   (1) The state financially supports and values education.
   (2) The state previously over-funded the education system.
   (3) Funding favors the elderly.
   (4) Funding favors areas that produce revenue rather than those that provide a public service.
   (5) The state's road system requires extensive repair.

2. What is most likely to happen to the education system if it is currently using all funding provided?

   (1) The state will no longer be able to build schools.
   (2) Schools will be unaffected by budget changes.
   (3) The state will not be able to cut the education budgets.
   (4) Schools will not be able to operate.
   (5) Classes may be larger and programs may have to be cancelled.

3. Which of the following is the most likely intended effect of the $428.3 million the state is adding to the budget for tax incentives?

   (1) Taxpayers will be taxed to produce the required funding.
   (2) State taxpayers will receive economic stimulus checks.
   (3) There will be increased private investment in schools.
   (4) New business construction will begin.
   (5) The number of business investments and the jobs that follow will increase.

4. Which of the following conclusions can be drawn from the information in the table?

   (1) The state is attempting to jump-start its economy.
   (2) The state is not attempting to balance the budget.
   (3) The state has a progressive educational system.
   (4) The state is levying additional taxes.
   (5) The state is cutting funding to all programs.

TIP

When you apply information from a table or chart, be sure you first understand the relationships of the facts stated or implied.

Questions 5 through 8 refer to the following chart.

Major Funding Sources for State and Local Government Projects	
Type of Funding	**Description**
Categorical grants-in-aid	federal money given to a state or local government for an approved, specific, narrowly-defined program. Spending is limited to the purpose stated in the grant. States are required to provide enough money to match a certain percent of the federal money.
Block grants	federal money given to a state government for a group of related categorical grants. State spending within the large program is less restricted.
Taxes	state and local money raised through taxes determined by each state and local government. These taxes can include state income taxes, sales taxes, property taxes, and license fees.
General revenue sharing	federal money given to a state government with only two restrictions on how the state spends the money. The money cannot be substituted for state aid to local governments, nor can it be used for any program that discriminates on the basis of race, national origin, or sex.
Special revenue sharing	federal money given to local governments for specific purposes such as: environmental protection, public safety, libraries, services for the poor and aged, and public transportation

5. Without federal money, what would states probably do?

(1) cut back on programs
(2) be financially independent
(3) increase their dependence on block grants
(4) eliminate local libraries
(5) have better public transportation

6. Which of the following is money that is raised locally?

(1) special revenue sharing
(2) taxes
(3) block grants
(4) categorical grants-in-aid
(5) general revenue sharing

7. A college town in Oregon has tripled in size over the last ten years. Townspeople, students, faculty, and college administrators asked the mayor to find funding for a bus system. The mayor received federal money, and the city did not have to spend anything on the new bus system. Which funding source did the mayor probably use?

(1) a categorical grant-in-aid
(2) a block grant
(3) taxes
(4) general revenue sharing
(5) special revenue sharing

8. A state needed additional money to help set up a job training. The state applied for and received money under a federal job training program but was required to contribute a portion of the funding itself. Which funding source was probably used?

(1) a categorical grant-in-aid
(2) a block grant
(3) taxes
(4) special revenue sharing
(5) general revenue sharing

Answers and explanations start on page 115.

Tables and Graphs

Bar Graphs

Some GED Social Studies Test questions may ask you about the information displayed in **bar graphs**. When reading a bar graph, determine what each bar on the graph represents and then compare the data by comparing the bars. A bar graph may contain a legend, or key, and a scale to help you interpret the value represented by each bar.

Look carefully at the bar graph. Choose the <u>one best answer</u> to the question.

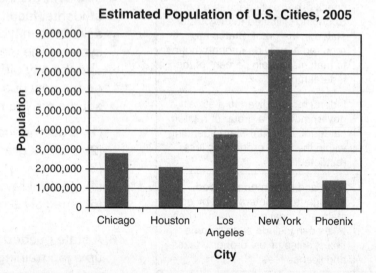

Estimated Population of U.S. Cities, 2005

QUESTION: Which of the following <u>best</u> summarizes the information in this graph?

(1) More people like New York than any other city in the United States.

(2) More people visit New York than any other city in the United States.

(3) The estimated population of New York is more than the combined populations of Chicago, Houston, Los Angeles, and Phoenix.

(4) The estimated population of New York is far greater than that of other large cities in the United States.

(5) New York has more residents per square mile than any other city.

EXPLANATIONS

STEP 1 To answer this question, ask yourself:

- What is this graph about? <u>the estimated populations of the five most populous cities in the United States in 2005</u>
- What is the question asking me to do? <u>Choose the statement that best summarizes the graph.</u>

STEP 2 Evaluate all of the answer choices and choose the <u>best</u> answer.

(1) No. The graph doesn't state information about people's opinions of the cities.

(2) No. The graph does not give information about visitors.

(3) No. According to the graph, the estimated population of New York is just over 8 million people, which is less than the combined populations of the other cities.

(4) **Yes. The bar representing the population of New York is far higher than the other bars, which means New York has the largest population.**

(5) No. The graph gives no information about population per square mile.

ANSWER: (4) The estimated population of New York is far greater than that of other large cities in the United States.

Practice the Skill

Try these examples. Choose the **one best answer** to each question. Then check your answers and read the explanations.

Imports and Exports of Selected Countries

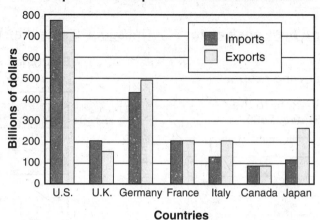

1. Which two nations export approximately the same value of goods?

   (1) The U.K. and France
   (2) France and Canada
   (3) France and Italy
   (4) Italy and Japan
   (5) The U.S. and Germany

   HINT For which two nations are the bars representing exports at similar heights?

2. Which of the following restates information from the graph?

   (1) The U.K., France, and Italy import approximately the same value of goods.
   (2) The value difference between imports and exports is greatest in Japan.
   (3) Only Japan exports more than the U.K.
   (4) The value of imports to the U.S. is twice that for Germany.
   (5) The U.S. exports more than it imports.

   HINT Which statement is true according to the graph?

Answers and Explanations

1. (3) France and Italy
Option (3) is correct because both France and Italy export approximately $200 billion worth of goods.

Options (1) and (4) are incorrect because for these answer pairs the graph shows similar values in imports, not exports. Options (2) and (5) are incorrect because for these answer pairs the graph shows nations with significantly different dollar values for exports.

2. (2) The value difference between imports and exports is greatest in Japan.
Option (2) is correct because the difference in height of the bars representing imports and exports in Japan is greater than that for any other nation.

Option (1) is incorrect because the value of imports to Italy is less than the value of imports to France and the U.K. Option (3) is incorrect because the graph shows that many nations export more than the U.K. Option (4) is incorrect because the value of imports to Germany is more than half the value of imports to the U.S. Option (5) is incorrect because the U.S. imports more goods than it exports.

Bar Graphs

Directions: Choose the **one best answer** to each question.

Questions 1 refers to the following graph.

Overseas Visitors to the United States, 2006

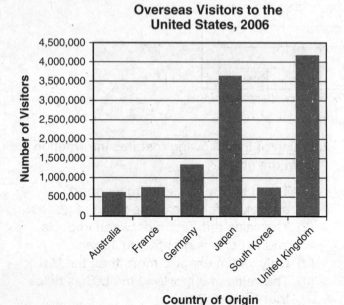

Country of Origin

1. Which of the following conclusions could you draw from the graph?

(1) Australians prefer to travel to countries other than the United States.
(2) The distance between Japan and the United States does not prevent millions of Japanese from traveling here.
(3) People from the United Kingdom prefer to visit the United States because Americans speak English.
(4) Most visitors from Japan and the United Kingdom are here for business.
(5) Germans and French visit other countries more than they do the United States.

Questions 2 and 3 refer to the following graph.

Estimated Population of California by Subgroup, 2006

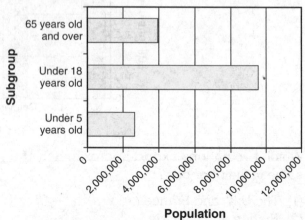

Population

2. What additional information is needed to determine the total estimated population of California in 2006?

(1) the total population between 18 and 65 years old
(2) the total population between 5 and 18 years old
(3) the total population that moved to California in 2006
(4) the total population that moved away from California in 2006
(5) the total number of births in California in 2006

3. Which of the following statements is supported by the graph?

(1) California has a high birth rate.
(2) More retirees live in California than other states.
(3) The population of California is likely to decline in years to come.
(4) Young people deserve attention in California.
(5) The population 65 and over is likely to double over the next two decades.

Questions 4 and 5 refer to the following graph.

Average grade that the public would give the public schools in their community and in the nation at large, 2007

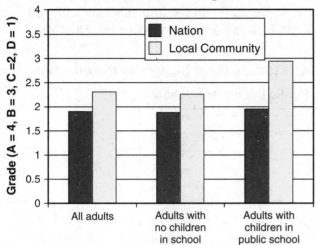

4. What average grade would all adults give to public schools in the nation at large?

(1) nearly an A
(2) nearly a B
(3) just above a C
(4) nearly a C
(5) just above a D

5. Which of the following best summarizes information in the graph?

(1) Adults with children in public school have a lower opinion of public schools than adults with no children in school.
(2) Adults generally believe that private schools are better than public schools.
(3) Adults generally have a higher opinion of local schools than of schools in the nation at large.
(4) More adults have children in public school than do not.
(5) More adults have children in private school than public school.

Questions 6 and 7 refer to the following graph.

Energy Consumption in the United States

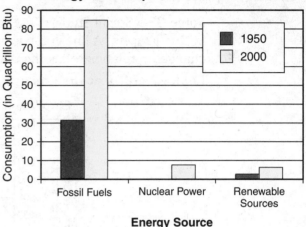

6. Which of the following restates information from the graph?

(1) The consumption of energy from fossil fuels in 2000 would have been four times that in 1950 if renewable sources were not available.
(2) Energy consumption from fossil fuels in 2000 would have been four times that in 1950 if not for conservation efforts.
(3) A negligible source of energy in 1950, nuclear power was the source of more energy than renewable sources in 2000.
(4) Energy consumption from renewable sources tripled from 1950 to 2000.
(5) The consumption of energy from fossil fuels tripled from 1950 to 2000.

7. Information in the graph could be used to support which of the following statements?

(1) The attempt to decrease the use of fossil fuels in favor of renewable sources has failed.
(2) Energy consumption from all sources more than doubled from 1950 to 2000.
(3) Nuclear power is a more reliable source of energy than renewable sources.
(4) Nuclear power is likely to replace fossil fuels as a source of energy.
(5) In future years, energy consumption from fossil fuels is likely to decline.

TIP

When studying bar graphs, ask:
• What is the subject of the graph?
• What does each bar represent?

Answers and explanations start on page 116.

KEY
Skill
13

Line Graphs

Some GED Social Studies Test questions may be based on the information displayed in **line graphs**. A line graph is used to show how the amount or value of something changes in relation to another variable.

Look carefully at the line graph. Choose the <u>one best answer</u> to the question.

Enrollment in U.S. Public Secondary Schools

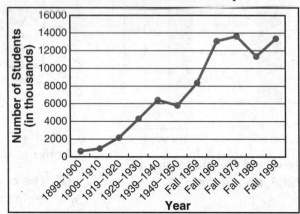

QUESTION: Which of the following <u>best</u> summarizes the information in this graph?

(1) The percentage of the U.S. population enrolled in public secondary schools increased through the twentieth century.

(2) Public secondary schools became more popular than private secondary schools through the twentieth century.

(3) The number of students enrolled in public secondary schools in the U.S. increased through the twentieth century.

(4) Students became increasingly better educated through the twentieth century.

(5) The number of students who went on to college in the U.S. increased through the twentieth century.

EXPLANATIONS

STEP 1 To answer this question, ask yourself:

• What does this graph show? <u>the enrollment in public secondary schools through the twentieth century</u>

• What is the question asking me to do? <u>Identify a statement that sums up the information in the graph.</u>

STEP 2 Evaluate all of the answer choices and choose the <u>best</u> answer.

(1) No. The graph shows number of students, not percent of the population.

(2) No. The graph gives no information about private school enrollment.

(3) Yes. The graph shows the number of students enrolled in public secondary schools generally increased in the twentieth century.

(4) No. The graph gives no information about the quality of education.

(5) No. The graph gives no information about college enrollment.

ANSWER: (3) The number of students enrolled in public secondary schools in the U.S. increased through the twentieth century.

Practice the Skill

Try these examples. Choose the <u>one best answer</u> to each question. Then check your answers and the explanations.

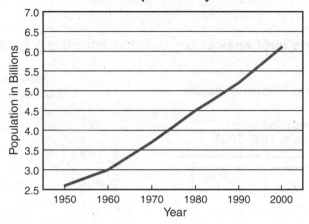

World Population by Decade

1. Which of the following restates information from the graph?

   (1) The world's rapid population growth has occurred primarily in third world countries.
   (2) The world's population has slowly increased over the past fifty years.
   (3) The world's population has remained static over the past fifty years.
   (4) The world's population has more than doubled since 1960.
   (5) The world's food supply will not be able to keep up with the rapid growth in population.

   HINT Which statement is based on facts given in the graph?

2. The rate of population growth depends on birth rates and life expectancy. Which of the following could most directly affect the continuation of the trend shown in the graph?

   (1) Worldwide, the sea level has already risen 4 to 8 inches.
   (2) Today, families are having half as many children as they did in the 1960s.
   (3) Modern agricultural techniques can produce more food than in the past.
   (4) Large parts of Africa and Asia suffer from shortages of clean water.
   (5) By 2100, the average temperature may increase by between 2.5 and 10.4 degrees Fahrenheit.

   HINT Which fact could most directly affect the trend shown on the graph?

Answers and Explanations

1. (4) The world's population has more than doubled since 1960.
Only option (4) correctly restates information given in the graph.

Options (1) and (5) are statements not supported by the graph, which gives no information about population growth in third world countries or the world's food supply. Options (2) and (3) contradict the data.

2. (2) Today, families are having half as many children as they did in the 1960s.
The graph shows the world's population increasing rapidly. Only option (2) states a fact that could directly affect the rate at which the world's population is increasing.

Options (1), (3), (4), and (5) state facts that could affect life expectancy but do not directly affect the rate at which the world's population increases.

Line Graphs

Directions: Choose the <u>one best answer</u> to each question.

Questions 1 and 2 refer to the following graph.

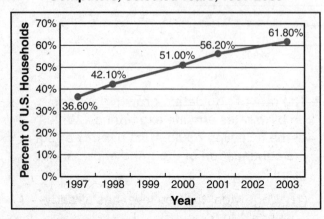

Percent of U.S. Households with Computers, Selected Years, 1997-2003

Questions 3 and 4 refer to the following graph.

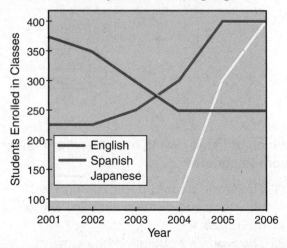

Adult Education Center Survey of Native Languages

1. Which of the following restates information from the graph?

   (1) The percent of homes with computers doubled from 1997 to 2003.
   (2) The greatest increase in the percent of households with computers was between 2000 and 2001.
   (3) No households purchased computers for the first time in 1999.
   (4) Between 1997 and 2003, computers became less expensive to purchase.
   (5) The percent of households with computers has increased each year since 1997.

2. Which of the following would be found if the trend in the graph continued past 2003?

   The percentage of U.S. households owning computers

   (1) increased for a year before decreasing
   (2) decreased for a year or two before increasing again
   (3) increased steadily
   (4) began to decline
   (5) peaked at 65% and remained steady

3. Which year saw the greatest increase in students whose native language was other than English?

   (1) 2001
   (2) 2002
   (3) 2003
   (4) 2004
   (5) 2005

4. Which of the following conclusions could you draw about the center?

   (1) There are no English-speaking students enrolled.
   (2) The center must address the needs of students whose native language is not English.
   (3) Unemployment rates have caused a decrease in English-speaking students.
   (4) Enrollment at the local community college must have increased.
   (5) The center has increased its class offerings for native English speakers.

Questions 5 and 6 refer to the following graph.

Jefferson County Solid Waste Department

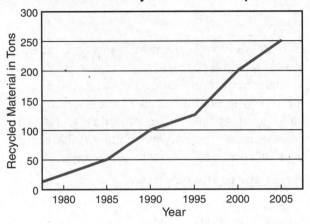

5. If recycling continues to increase at the same rate as it did between 2000 and 2005, approximately how much material will be recycled in 2010?

   (1) 250 tons
   (2) 300 tons
   (3) 350 tons
   (4) 400 tons
   (5) 450 tons

6. County leaders want to know whether the trend shown in the graph means that the individual citizens of the county are recycling more in 2005 than they did in 1980. What additional information do they need?

   (1) the amount in tons of garbage thrown away in Jefferson County in 2005
   (2) the amount in tons of material recycled statewide in 2005
   (3) the rate at which recycling increased from 1980 through 2005 in neighboring Hammond County
   (4) the rate at which the amount of garbage thrown away increased from 1980 through 2005
   (5) the population of the county in 2005 as compared to the population in 1980

Question 7 refers to the following graph.

6-Year Comparison of Utility Bills in Charleston and Kershaw Counties

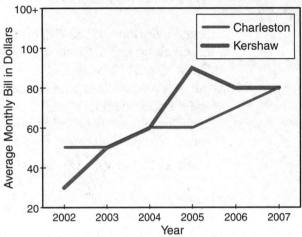

7. What conclusion can you draw based on the information provided in the graph?

   (1) The cost of living is higher in Charleston County.
   (2) The cost of living is higher in Kershaw County.
   (3) Kershaw County was able to reduce its utility rates.
   (4) Charleston County utility rates did not cover the cost to provide electricity to everyone's home.
   (5) Kershaw County utility charges dropped only when people complained.

TIP

Look at the axes to understand the relationship being illustrated. A line graph can depict upward, downward, or static trends. To interpret the information, locate specific points on the graph and identify the trend shown.

Answers and explanations start on page 116.

Tables and Graphs

Circle Graphs

Some questions on the GED Social Studies Test will have you answer questions based on **circle graphs.** Circle graphs are used to represent a part-to-whole relationship. Circle graphs show, at a glance, the relative sizes of different categories that make up parts of a whole. Because the sections of a circle graph can be seen as representing slices of an imaginary pie, circle graphs are also sometimes called **pie charts.** Not all circle graphs show percentages, but a complete circle graph always equals 100% of the topic—or "pie"—it refers to, with each sector representing a certain percentage.

Look at the graph. Choose the <u>one best answer</u> to the question.

U.S. Population,
Coastal vs. Inland Counties

U.S Population residing in Inland Counties 47%

U.S Population residing in Coastal Counties 53%

QUESTION: Which of the following restates information from the graph?

   (1) A majority of U.S. residents live far from the oceans.
   (2) Because of international trade, most U.S. cities are located along coastlines.
   (3) A majority of U.S. residents do not live in coastal counties.
   (4) Global warming could result in rising sea levels, affecting coastal counties.
   (5) A majority of U.S. residents live in counties along coastlines.

EXPLANATIONS

STEP 1   To answer this question, ask yourself:

   • What is the graph about? <u>the proportion of U.S. residents who live in coastal and inland counties</u>
   • What is the question asking me to do? <u>Choose the statement that restates information from the graph.</u>

STEP 2   Evaluate all of the answer choices and choose the <u>best</u> answer.

   (1) No. This option is incorrect and the opposite of the correct answer.
   (2) No. This is an opinion that is not supported by the graph.
   (3) No. This option is incorrect and the opposite of the correct answer.
   (4) No. While it may be true, this option identifies a cause and effect that is not supported by the graph.
   (5) Yes. The graph shows that more than half, a majority, of U.S. residents live in coastal counties.

ANSWER: (5) A majority of U.S. residents live in counties along coastlines.

Practice the Skill

Try these examples. Choose the <u>one best answer</u> to each question. Then check your answers and the explanations.

**Use of Carrier Pigeons
During the 1870 Siege of Paris**

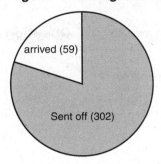

arrived (59)

Sent off (302)

1. During the siege of Paris in 1870, carrier pigeons were used to break the blockade.

   Which of the following <u>best</u> restates information from the graph?

   (1) A carrier pigeon is a racing pigeon trained to return home.
   (2) About one in ten carrier pigeons succeeded in breaking the blockade.
   (3) The pigeon should be incorporated into the coat of arms of Paris.
   (4) About 20% of the carrier pigeons sent to Paris arrived with their messages.
   (5) Carrier pigeons were useful because tiny messages could be delivered embedded in their wings.

   HINT Which best restates the main idea of the graph?

2. Which of the following is an assumption made by the graph?

   (1) Carrier pigeons carried information to the people of Paris from the outside world.
   (2) Carrier pigeons had never been used before.
   (3) Approximately 1 in 5 of the carrier pigeons sent arrived in Paris.
   (4) Almost 60 pigeons succeeded.
   (5) None of the above.

   HINT What does the graph assume you already know about carrier pigeons?

Answers and Explanations

1. (4) About 20% of the carrier pigeons sent to Paris arrived with their messages.
Option (4) is correct because it identifies the main idea of the graph, which is that about 1 in 5, or 20%, of the carrier pigeons sent to Paris arrived.

While options (1) and (5) are true, these options are incorrect because they don't restate information provided in the graph. Option (2) is contradicted by the numbers shown in the graph. That the pigeon should be used in Paris's coat of arms (option 3) is an opinion, not an idea stated in the graph.

2. (1) Carrier pigeons carried information to the people of Paris from the outside world.
Option (1) is correct; although the graph does not state this as the purpose of the carrier pigeon flights, the assumption is that the reader understands this.

Information about carrier pigeons' previous use (option 2) is not included in the graph. The facts that about 1 in 5 pigeons sent arrived in the city (option 3), or almost 60 total (option 4), are incorrect choices because they are not assumptions but rather are clearly stated in the graph. Option (5) is incorrect because option (1) is a valid assumption made by the graph.

Circle Graphs

Directions: Choose the **one best answer** to each question.

Question 1 refers to the following graphs.

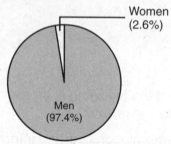

Female Executives in Fortune 500 Companies

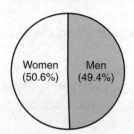

Women in Management, Professional, and Related Occupations

1. Which of the following conclusions can be drawn from the two graphs?

   (1) Women have come a long way to be able to serve as chief executives.
   (2) Women do not make good executives.
   (3) There is a strong gender prejudice in top companies.
   (4) Though they make up half of the management force in today's business world, women are underrepresented in the executive jobs at top companies.
   (5) Women would make the best executives if only given the chance.

Question 2 refers to the following graphs.

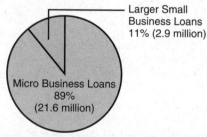

Number of Small Business Loans in 2006

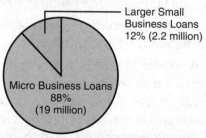

Number of Small Business Loans in 2007

2. Micro business loans are less than $100,000. Loans in the $100,000-to-$1 million category are larger small business loans.

   Which of the following conclusions **best** restates information about changes in micro business loans from 2006 to 2007?

   (1) The number of micro business loans fell from 21.6 million in 2006 to 19 million in 2007.
   (2) Micro business loans can be a good way to help finance a small business.
   (3) The number of micro business loans grew significantly from 2006 to 2007.
   (4) Micro business loans were taken out by small-business owners.
   (5) Micro business loans were pretty much the same for 2006 and 2007.

TIP

In studying circle graphs, ask the following questions: What does the entire circle represent? What do the parts of the circle represent?

Questions 3 through 6 refer to the following passage and graphs.

The Election of 1824

Election results have often been controversial. One such election was the presidential election of 1824. Four candidates were on the ballot—Andrew Jackson, Henry Clay, John Quincy Adams, and William Crawford. Andrew Jackson won the most popular votes but failed to win a clear majority and did not have enough electoral votes to win. Clay urged his supporters to cast their electoral votes for Adams, who was elected president. An important outcome of the election was that Jackson and his supporters joined together to form the Democratic Party and campaigned among workers and farmers who had not previously voted. This effort with the "common" man helped Jackson defeat Adams in 1828 to win the presidential election.

The Election of 1824

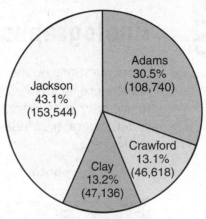

Popular Vote

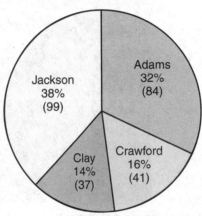

Electoral Vote

3. Which of the following statements is most relevant to the outcome of the 1824 election?

   (1) No candidate won at least 50% of the popular vote.
   (2) Two hundred and sixty-one electoral votes were cast in the 1824 election.
   (3) All of the candidates were part of the same political party.
   (4) Both popular and electoral votes have always been used in election results.
   (5) Four candidates were contenders in the 1824 presidential election.

4. How many electoral votes did Adams receive from Clay?

   (1) 47,136
   (2) 46,618
   (3) 41
   (4) 37
   (5) 14

5. How many total electoral votes were possible in the 1824 election?

   (1) 356,040
   (2) 261
   (3) 121
   (4) 99
   (5) 84

6. Which of the following conclusions can be drawn about presidential elections?

   (1) The candidate with the highest popular vote always becomes president.
   (2) The popular vote determines the number of electoral votes received.
   (3) The Electoral College makes the final decision on presidential elections.
   (4) Plurality of the popular vote is more important than majority of popular vote.
   (5) Presidential elections are never won by the individual with the majority of the popular vote.

Answers and explanations start on page 117.

Skill 15

Photographs

Some questions on the GED Social Studies Test will ask you to look at a **photograph** and choose an answer based on information in the photograph. You may be asked to use prior knowledge, draw conclusions, or identify implications. The information in a photograph includes the title, caption, or any other text that accompanies the photograph.

Look at the photograph. Choose the <u>one best answer</u> to the question.

QUESTION:
What change in U.S. law attempted to prevent the situation depicted in the photograph?

(1) establishment of a minimum wage
(2) recognition of labor unions
(3) creation of a social security system
(4) institution of child labor laws
(5) state-supported education

EXPLANATIONS

STEP 1 To answer this question, ask yourself:

- What is this a photograph of? <u>a young girl working in a factory in the early twentieth century</u>
- What is the question asking me to do? <u>Identify the change in U.S. law that tried to stop factory owners from using children as workers.</u>

STEP 2 Evaluate all of the answer choices and choose the <u>best</u> answer.

(1) No. A minimum wage might improve the conditions for all workers, but this is not the best option for preventing the situation in the photograph.
(2) No. Labor unions might fight for the rights of all workers, but this is not the best option for preventing the situation in the photograph.
(3) No. Creation of a social security system would not change the situation in the photograph.
(4) Yes. The creation of child labor laws would prevent children like the girl shown in the photograph from having to work in factories.
(5) No. Creation of state-supported education would not stop the situation in the photograph.

ANSWER: (4) institution of child labor laws

Practice the Skill

Try these examples. Choose the one best answer to each question. Then check your answers and the explanations.

1. From the photograph, what conclusion can you draw about the people who live in a suburb?

   They are comfortable with

   (1) individuality.
   (2) isolation.
   (3) excitement.
   (4) conformity.
   (5) democracy.

   HINT Which option would be necessary for people who live in a home that looks just like that of their neighbors?

2. Which trends in the post–World War II period are reflected in the photograph?

   (1) development of cars and suburbs
   (2) returning soldiers with many injuries
   (3) hand-crafted construction techniques
   (4) the public's need for privacy and security
   (5) returning soldiers in need of housing and development of mass-production

   HINT Which option best reflects trends that resulted in the subject of the photograph?

Answers and Explanations

1. (4) conformity.
Option (4) is the best answer; people who live where all the houses look the same must be comfortable doing things the same way as everyone else.

Options (1) and (2) are both opposites of the correct answer; the neighborhood in the photograph would allow little room for individuality or isolation. While the people who live in a suburb may value excitement (option 3) and democracy (option 5), the photograph does not address these concepts.

2. (5) returning soldiers in need of housing and development of mass-production
The sharp rise in the number of returning soldiers who needed places to live and start families resulted in new processes that could produce houses of similar look and quality in a short amount of time (option 5).

While suburbs did develop, cars were not a new trend in the photograph (option 1). Soldiers' injuries are not portrayed in the photograph (option 2). Option (3) is the opposite of the mass-produced, similar-looking houses in the photograph. The suburb in the photograph would not have given residents privacy (option 4).

Photographs

Directions: Choose the one best answer to each question.

Questions 1 and 2 refer to the following photograph.

President Roosevelt signs the declaration of war against Japan.

1. Based on the photograph and caption, which of the following American policies related to the U.S. involvement in World War II did Roosevelt change?

   (1) Truman Doctrine
   (2) immigration laws
   (3) isolationism
   (4) military benefits
   (5) financial support for education

2. Which of the following had an immediate impact on the American economy as a result of the declaration of war on Japan?

   (1) increased military costs
   (2) decreased military costs
   (3) increased housing costs
   (4) increased education costs
   (5) decreased education costs

Questions 3 and 4 refer to the following photograph.

The New Workforce

3. Which of the following statements is best supported by the photograph and caption?

   (1) Women with children must work in order to maintain a middle class lifestyle.
   (2) A major social issue in today's workforce is balancing a career with family.
   (3) Women are happier being part of the workforce than raising families.
   (4) Today's workforce has not changed since World War II.
   (5) Most women today are employed in managerial or factory positions.

4. Many businesses would rather keep veteran employees than recruit and train new ones. Based on this information and the photograph, which of the following might best help do that?

   (1) providing onsite daycare
   (2) restricting family leave to increase wages
   (3) requiring more overtime
   (4) increasing insurance costs to improve family coverage
   (5) providing mentors for male employees

Questions 5 and 6 refer to the following photograph.

5. If the woman in the photograph is an employee of Mid City Realty, what does she most likely want from her employer?

  (1) higher hourly pay
  (2) fewer hours
  (3) end of discrimination
  (4) better working conditions
  (5) more health insurance

6. Which of the following does the photograph best illustrate?

  (1) rioting
  (2) lobbying
  (3) picketing
  (4) meeting
  (5) boycotting

> **TIP**
>
> When you answer questions based on photographs, first identify the subject, time, and significance of the photograph.

Questions 7 and 8 refer to the following photograph.

A group of West Germans peer over the infamous Berlin Wall.

7. For more than 50 years, the Berlin Wall separated communist East Berlin from democratic West Berlin. What did the Berlin Wall symbolize to the world?

  (1) oppression versus freedom
  (2) acceptance of cultural diversity
  (3) the end of World War II
  (4) free trade
  (5) open-door relations among nations

8. Which generalization about the experience of East and West Berliners under a divided Berlin is best supported by the photograph?

East and West Berliners

  (1) could move freely to and from each other's part of the city
  (2) wore scarves if they were women and suits if they were men
  (3) could not move freely to and from each other's part of the city
  (4) often tried to climb over the Berlin Wall
  (5) were often shot trying to cross over the Berlin Wall

Answers and explanations start on page 117.

Illustrations

Timelines and Drawings

Some questions on the GED Social Studies Test will ask you to look at timelines and drawings. **Timelines** provide short representations of events over a specified period of time. Information can be gathered not only from the dates, but also from the title and any additional information that connects the events to specific time periods.

A **drawing** is a visual representation of a subject. Drawings often include very specific details. They can be visual aids to understanding information presented in a passage.

Look at the drawing. Choose the <u>one best answer</u> to the question.

Trade Balance

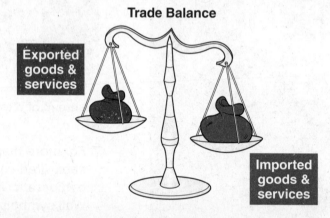

QUESTION: Each year the United States imports and exports billions of dollars worth of goods and services. A trade deficit occurs when there is an imbalance between exports and imports. Based on the drawing, what would the U.S. need to do to fix its trade deficit?

(1) purchase more services from other countries
(2) produce more goods for sale in the United States
(3) provide more services to Americans living in foreign countries
(4) reduce export of goods and services to other countries
(5) increase the amount of exports to other countries

EXPLANATIONS

STEP 1

To answer this question, ask yourself:

- What is this drawing about? <u>trade balance between imports and exports</u>
- What is the question asking me to do? <u>Draw a conclusion, based on the drawing, about the action the U.S. should take to achieve a balance of trade.</u>

STEP 2

Evaluate all of the answer choices and choose the <u>best</u> answer.

(1) No. Purchasing more from other countries would increase imports.
(2) No. Goods sold in the U.S. are not factors in international trade.
(3) No. Services for Americans living in foreign countries are not factors in trade.
(4) No. Reducing exports would increase the trade imbalance.
(5) Yes. The scales in the drawing show an imbalance in favor of imported goods and services. To correct the imbalance, the U.S. would need to increase exported goods and services.

ANSWER: (5) increase the amount of exports to other countries

Practice the Skill

Try these examples. Choose the <u>one best answer</u> to each question. Then check your answers and the explanations.

Struggle Toward Suffrage

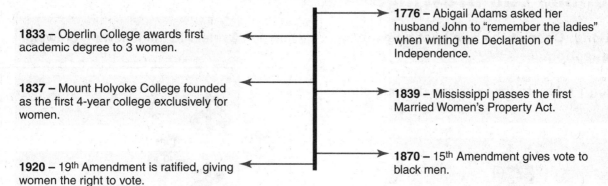

1833 – Oberlin College awards first academic degree to 3 women.

1776 – Abigail Adams asked her husband John to "remember the ladies" when writing the Declaration of Independence.

1837 – Mount Holyoke College founded as the first 4-year college exclusively for women.

1839 – Mississippi passes the first Married Women's Property Act.

1920 – 19th Amendment is ratified, giving women the right to vote.

1870 – 15th Amendment gives vote to black men.

1. Which statement does the timeline support?

   (1) Colleges for women were begun years before they gained the right to vote.
   (2) It was more difficult for black men to earn the right to vote than for women.
   (3) The 19th Amendment would have been ratified earlier if more women had supported it.
   (4) In the 1800s, women were only allowed to enroll in female-only colleges.
   (5) The Married Women's Property Act was a result of the 19th amendment.

   HINT Which option <u>best</u> restates information from the timeline?

2. Which event might male and female Suffragists have seen as not successful enough?

   (1) the passage of the first Married Women's Property Act
   (2) Oberlin College awarding academic degrees to 3 women
   (3) the ratification of the 15th Amendment
   (4) Abigail Adams's reminding her husband to remember the ladies
   (5) none of the above

   HINT Which event would Suffragists have seen as good but not good enough?

Answers and Explanations

1. (1) Colleges for women were begun years before they gained the right to vote.

Option (1) is correct because the first college for women was founded in 1837; women didn't gain the right to vote until 1920.

Option (2) is contradicted by the table; black men earned the right to vote in 1870, women in 1920. The timeline does not indicate how much support the 19th Amendment had (option 3). Option (4) is contradicted by the timeline; women received degrees from Oberlin College in 1833, but the first all-female college wasn't founded until 1837. Mississippi's Married Women's Property Act came before the 19th amendment was ratified (option 5), so it was not a result.

2. (3) the ratification of the 15th Amendment

Option (3) is correct. Suffragists felt that the 15th Amendment did not go far enough to extend the vote to all adults—men and women.

Options (1), (2), and (4) are incorrect because none of them relates to the interests of both men and women. Option (5) is incorrect because option (3) addresses the question.

Timelines and Drawings

Directions: Choose the one best answer to each question.

Question 1 refers to the following drawing.

The Far West—shooting buffalo on the line of the Kansas-Pacific Railroad

1. Which of the following statements is <u>best</u> supported by this drawing from the late 1800s?

   (1) Indians did not hunt buffalo.
   (2) Buffalo were killed for food.
   (3) Buffalo were killed as white civilization moved westward.
   (4) Buffalo are extinct today.
   (5) Buffalo are indigenous to Montana.

Question 2 refers to the following drawing.

2. Which of the following conclusions is implied by the drawing?

   (1) If you drive a car, you'll make more money than if you drive a moped.
   (2) Mopeds are more expensive than cars.
   (3) You can't buy a car if you have bad credit.
   (4) Very few people can afford to drive cars.
   (5) Cars cost more to drive than mopeds.

TIP

Always read the title and any captions or labels on drawings. They may provide details needed to answer questions.

World War I, 1914–1919

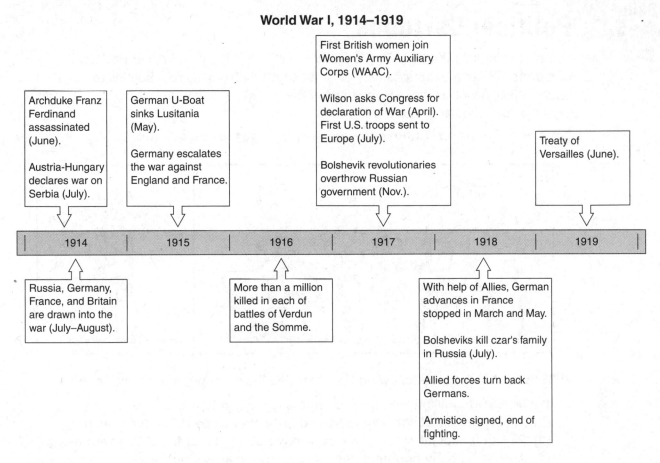

3. Which of the following might have resulted from Austria-Hungary declaring war on Serbia in July 1914?

   (1) The United States was drawn into war.
   (2) The Russian government was overthrown by the Bolshevik Party.
   (3) Archduke Ferdinand was assassinated.
   (4) As an ally of Serbia, Russia mobilized its armies.
   (5) none of the above

4. Based on the information in the timeline, which of the following inferences is correct?

   (1) Women did not participate in the war.
   (2) The First World War was a time of great turmoil.
   (3) Verdun and the Somme were the bloodiest battles in history.
   (4) France and Germany were allies.
   (5) England and Germany were allies.

5. Which of the following restates information about the U.S. entering the war?

   (1) The U.S. was not involved in World War I.
   (2) The U.S. entered the war later than the other countries.
   (3) The U.S. entered the war before the other countries.
   (4) The U.S. entered the war after Wilson was criticized for not joining the fight.
   (5) Wilson was a Democrat.

6. Based on the timeline, what conclusion can you draw about the role of women in war?

   (1) Wars include men only.
   (2) Wars include both men and women.
   (3) Women did not take part in wars until World War II.
   (4) Women did not take part in wars until Vietnam.
   (5) In the future, only women will fight wars.

Answers and explanations start on page 118.

Illustrations

Political Cartoons

Some questions on the GED Social Studies Test will ask you to look at **political cartoons.** These illustrations can focus on anything from current politics to social issues. Always look at the cartoon in its entirety and consider everything the cartoon is saying before choosing an answer option.

Look at the cartoon. Choose the <u>one best answer</u> to the question.

QUESTION: Which of the following best restates the main point of the cartoon?

    (1) In 2011, 76 million U.S. baby boomers will begin to retire.

    (2) Paying for social security will be no problem for the U.S. government.

    (3) Paying for social security will be a major obstacle for the U.S. government.

    (4) As long as baby boomers get social security, all will be well.

    (5) None of the above.

EXPLANATIONS

STEP 1

To answer this question, ask yourself:

- What is this cartoon about? <u>U.S. baby boomers who will begin receiving social security in 2011 and the economic problems that will result</u>
- What is the question asking me to do? <u>Choose the option that best puts the main idea of the cartoon into new words.</u>

STEP 2

Evaluate all of the answer choices and choose the <u>best</u> answer.

    (1) No. While it's true that baby boomers will begin to retire in 2011, this is only part of the main point of the cartoon.

    (2) No. This option is contradicted by the cartoon, which implies that paying for social security won't be easy by showing a confused Uncle Sam.

    (3) No. While paying for social security will be difficult, this is only one part of the cartoon's main idea.

    (4) No. The cartoon contradicts this idea by showing a desperate U.S.A. with his hand extended in need.

    (5) Yes. The main idea of the cartoon is that paying for social security is not only a problem in itself but will cause other problems as well, including an inability to pay for other services such as housing and transportation.

ANSWER: (5) None of the above.

Practice the Skill

1. From the cartoon, what can you infer about China's growing use of coal?

   (1) Chinese leadership wants the country to become more energy efficient.
   (2) By 2030, China's coal use could exceed that of all industrialized countries combined.
   (3) China should switch to nuclear power.
   (4) Coal use is not a problem for the Chinese.
   (5) All industrialized countries are polluters.

   HINT Which inference is most clearly seen in the cartoon?

2. Which option <u>best</u> explains the cause of the pollution expected to occur in China?

   (1) China has thousands of factories fueled by coal.
   (2) In 2006, a heavy cloud of pollutants over Northern China drifted to Seoul, Korea.
   (3) China must clean up its coal plants.
   (4) Increased global warming is the source of increasing pollution in China.
   (5) Pollution from other countries is increasing China's pollution.

   HINT Which cause explains the increased pollution expected in China in the coming years?

Answers and Explanations

1. **(2) By 2030, China's coal use could exceed that of all industrialized countries combined.**
Option (2) is correct; as the cartoon indicates, by 2030 China's pollution could be greater than that made by all the industrialized countries combined.

Options (1), (3), and (4) are incorrect because the cartoon doesn't address Chinese leaders, nuclear power, or how the Chinese feel about their pollution. While it's true the industrialized nations are also polluters (option 5), this isn't an inference about China's use of coal.

2. **(1) China has thousands of factories fueled by coal.**
Option (1) is correct because it clearly states the cause of the pollution problem.

Option (2) is an effect, not a cause of pollution. Option (3) is an opinion about China's responsibilities, not a cause of pollution. Option (4) is not logical and is contradicted by the cartoon. That pollution from other countries (option 5) is causing pollution in China is not indicated by the cartoon.

Political Cartoons

Directions: Choose the one best answer to each question.

Question 1 refers to the following cartoon.

1. Over time, the symbols of the elephant for the Republican Party and the donkey for the Democratic Party have become widely accepted by the public. Which of the following **best** summarizes the main idea of the cartoon?

   (1) The donkey is a negative symbol of the democrats, and the elephant a positive symbol of the republicans.
   (2) The elephant is always a negative symbol for the republicans.
   (3) The donkey is always a negative symbol for the democrats.
   (4) Voters believe the donkey is actually clever and courageous.
   (5) The meaning of the donkey and the elephant as political symbols depends upon the opinion of the audience.

Question 2 refers to the following text and cartoon.

"A Foot in Two Different Worlds"

North Korea today is a communist dictatorship, an isolated, destitute country cut off from modern technology and struggling with severe food shortages. South Korea is a capitalist democracy, a manufacturing dynamo now embracing the digital economy.

2. Which of the following is implied by the cartoon?

   (1) Korea is both stuck in the past and trying to move toward the future.
   (2) Korea is a giant ready to take on the world.
   (3) North Korea's nuclear capacity is a grave concern of its enemies.
   (4) South Korea is not able to feed its own people.
   (5) North Korea is wealthy.

Questions 3 through 5 refer to the following cartoon.

HAVING CHOICES CAN BE HABIT FORMING.

IF THESE ARE MY ONLY CHOICES,
I'LL NEVER VOTE.

IF I HAVE ALL THESE CHOICES,
I'LL ALWAYS VOTE.

3. What can you infer about the cartoonist's attitude toward the young people shown?

   (1) They should stop being so picky.
   (2) Young people deserve to be addressed and engaged by the political process.
   (3) Young people ages 18 to 21 have never been a major voting bloc.
   (4) Young voters are too emotional.
   (5) Young voters are likely to be democrats.

4. Which assumption best supports the information in the cartoons?

   (1) If young voters are given inspiring choices in 2012, they will be back to vote in 2016.
   (2) Voters in 2012 won't vote in 2016.
   (3) Voter turnout depends on the candidates.
   (4) Democrats are always the same as Republicans.
   (5) Young people are not political anymore.

5. Which conclusion can you draw from the cartoons?

   (1) When young people are engaged in elections, they turn out to vote, but they may never vote again.
   (2) When young people are engaged in elections, they turn out to vote, and they will make a habit of voting in the future.
   (3) Young voters have power and can impact an election.
   (4) Even when young people are not faced with interesting choices, they will still turn out to vote.
   (5) Democrats and republicans don't hold the interest of young people.

TIP

To best "read" a cartoon, combine all the bits of information provided. The characters, layout, labels, and captions can all tell you something about the meaning of the cartoon.

Answers and explanations start on page 119.

Illustrations

Maps

Some questions on the GED Social Studies Test will ask you to look at **maps**. Maps are tools that can serve a variety of functions. Depending on the type of map, you may be able to find information about political borders, roads, elevations and land forms, weather and climate, historical events, or the distribution of population or resources. Information in maps can be found in titles, labels, dates, and keys.

Look at the map. Choose the <u>one best answer</u> to the question.

QUESTION: In the late 1800s, the steel industry grew rapidly. Steel production depended on three natural resources: iron, coal, and limestone. Which states each had two of the resources needed for steel production?

(1) Illinois and Pennsylvania
(2) Colorado and Wyoming
(3) Minnesota and Iowa
(4) Virginia and North Carolina
(5) New York and Pennsylvania

EXPLANATIONS

STEP 1 To answer this question, ask yourself:

• What is this map about? <u>geographic distribution of U.S. mineral resources</u>
• What is the question asking me to do? <u>Restate information from the map: which pair of states each had two of the natural resources needed to make steel?</u>

STEP 2 Evaluate all of the answer choices and choose the <u>best</u> answer.

(1) Yes. This option is correct because both Illinois and Pennsylvania had two of the resources needed for coal production—coal fields and limestone.
(2) No. While Colorado had coal and limestone, Wyoming had only coal fields.
(3) No. Iowa had only coal fields, and Minnesota had only iron ore.
(4) No. North Carolina had none, and Virginia had only limestone.
(5) No. New York had iron, and Pennsylvania had coal fields and limestone.

ANSWER: (1) Illinois and Pennsylvania

Practice the Skill

Try these examples. Choose the <u>one best answer</u> to each question. Then check your answers and the explanations.

Australia's Climate Zones

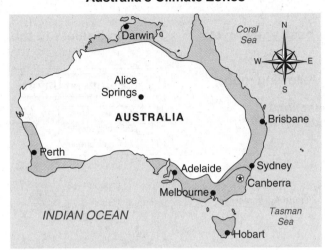

1. Based on the map, which of the following generalizations can you make about Australia's major cities?

   (1) Most major cities are located on the north coast of the continent.
   (2) Australia has no cities on its western coast.
   (3) Most major Australian cities are found along the coast.
   (4) None of the cities are located inland.
   (5) Some of Australia's major cities should be moved inland.

   HINT Which generalization is <u>best</u> supported by information found in the map?

2. Some important information for the map is missing. Which of the following would be most helpful in interpreting this map?

   (1) the date the map was created
   (2) a key for the map's colors
   (3) the location of mountains and rivers
   (4) the population of the cities
   (5) a compass rose

   HINT Which option would provide information that would help you understand the map?

Answers and Explanations

1. (3) Most major Australian cities are found along the coast.

Option (3) is correct; of the many cities shown, only Alice Springs is not located on the coast.

Option (1) is incorrect; the only city located on the north coast is Darwin. Option (2) is contradicted by the map, which shows Perth on the western coast. That none of the cities are located inland (option 4) is contradicted by the map, which shows the inland city of Alice Springs. Option (5) is incorrect because nothing on the map supports the idea that cities should be moved.

2. (2) a key for the map colors

Option (2) is correct. The map's title indicates that the colored areas on the map indicate different climate zones. A map key would be useful because it would indicate what climate zones the colored areas represent.

Options (1), (3), and (4) are not correct because none of these choices would help you understand the climate information on the map. Option (5) is incorrect because the map already includes a compass rose.

Maps

Directions: Choose the <u>one best answer</u> to each question.

Questions 1 and 2 refer to the following map.

**U.S. Imposes Economic Sanctions
Because of Drug Trade**

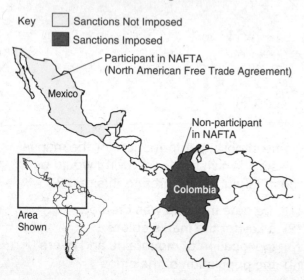

Question 3 refers to the following map.

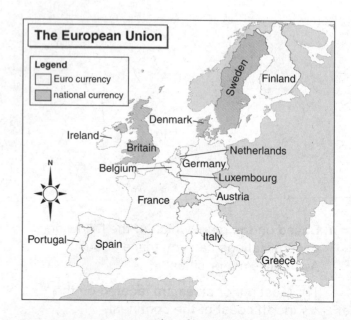

1. Both Mexico and Colombia are participants in the illicit drug trade that has brought many problems to the U.S. Which of the following is an opinion based on the map?

   (1) Sanctions were not applied to Mexico.
   (2) The drug trade is destructive to all countries.
   (3) Colombia is not a participant in NAFTA.
   (4) Sanctions were applied to Colombia.
   (5) Mexico is a participant in NAFTA.

2. Identify the implication suggested by the map.

   (1) There is more drug trade in Mexico than in Colombia.
   (2) There is more drug trade in Colombia than in Mexico.
   (3) Sanctions were not imposed on Colombia because the country is farther from the U.S.
   (4) Sanctions were imposed on Mexico because the country is closer to the U.S.
   (5) Sanctions were not imposed on Mexico because it is a participant in NAFTA.

3. Which of the following summarizes the main idea of the map?

   (1) Spain, France, and Germany use the Euro.
   (2) All European Union members use the Euro except Britain and Sweden, which retain their own national currencies.
   (3) All European Union members use the Euro except Denmark, Sweden, and Britain, which retain their own national currencies.
   (4) Sweden does not use the Euro.
   (5) All the major countries of Europe use the Euro.

Questions 4 through 7 refer to the following map of Brazil.

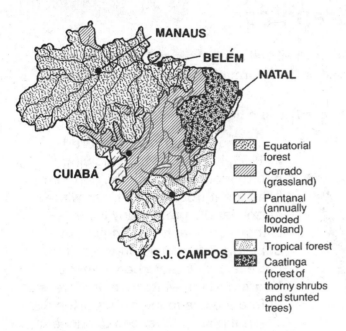

MANAUS
BELÉM
NATAL
CUIABÁ
S.J. CAMPOS

Equatorial forest

Cerrado (grassland)

Pantanal (annually flooded lowland)

Tropical forest

Caatinga (forest of thorny shrubs and stunted trees)

4. Which of the following can be determined from the map?

(1) the major agricultural products of Brazil
(2) Brazil's population densities
(3) the location of mountains and plateaus
(4) the location of mineral resources
(5) major patterns of vegetation

5. According to the map, which is probably the least desirable area of Brazil?

(1) equatorial forest
(2) Natal
(3) Manaus
(4) Cuiabá
(5) S. J. Campos

6. One of the world's largest hydroelectric (water-driven) plants can be found in the Parana-Paraguay-Plata river complex in the southwest region of Brazil, west of Cuiabá. What information from the map suggests that this area is suitable for hydroelectric plants?

(1) The equatorial forest surrounds the Amazon River.
(2) The Caatinga has vegetation that does not need much water.
(3) The Pantanal floods annually.
(4) Tropical forests contain a rich abundance of wildlife.
(5) The Cerrado supports agriculture.

7. What conclusion is supported by the map?

(1) Brazil is not a highly developed country.
(2) Brazil has few natural resources.
(3) Brazil's natural resources have not been fully utilized.
(4) There are only five major cities in Brazil.
(5) Brazil is larger than the United States.

TIP

It is important to know how to interpret common parts of maps.
• The title states the purpose of the map.
• The key or legend identifies the meaning of the symbols on the map.
• The compass rose shows directions on the map.

Answers and explanations start on page 119.

Combine Text and Graphics

Some questions on the GED Social Studies Test will ask you to read a passage and look at a graphic and answer questions based on the information included in both the text and the graphic.

Study the cartoon and passage. Choose the one best answer to the question.

WHEN WILL HE ADMIT THIS?

"WHY, THERE IS REALLY NO DIFFERENCE AT ALL."

When this cartoon appeared in 1905, it included the following information along with the caption: "The great trouble with most white people and a great many Negroes is they have been laboring under a delusion. The idea is prevalent that there is a difference between the Negro and the white man. If there is a difference it is found in Opportunity. Given the same chances to succeed, there is no difference at all."

QUESTION: According to the cartoon and passage, what was the cause of job inequality between African Americans and whites in 1905?

   (1) talent
   (2) opportunity
   (3) income
   (4) intelligence
   (5) rights

EXPLANATIONS

STEP 1 To answer this question, ask yourself:

- What are the cartoon and passage about? <u>The only real difference between blacks and whites is in the opportunity they were given to succeed in 1905.</u>
- What is the question asking me to do? <u>Identify the cause of job inequality between African Americans and whites in 1905.</u>

STEP 2 Evaluate all of the answer choices and choose the <u>best</u> answer.

   (1) No. The cartoon and passage don't mention talent as a factor.
   (2) Yes. The passage states the only thing limiting blacks' success in 1905 was opportunity.
   (3) No. The cartoon and passage don't mention income as a factor.
   (4) No. The cartoon and passage don't mention intelligence as a factor.
   (5) No. While rights are one aspect of equality, the main case of inequality noted in the cartoon and passage is lack of equal opportunity.

ANSWER: (2) opportunity

Practice the Skill

Try these examples. Choose the <u>one best answer</u> to each question. Then check your answers and read the explanations.

When groups of people who speak the same language become physically separated by barriers, such as large bodies of water, deserts, and mountains, small changes accumulate in their languages. Over time, the changes can lead to the use of different languages. Linguists group languages into families that can all be traced back to the common parent language that linguists call Proto-Indo-European.

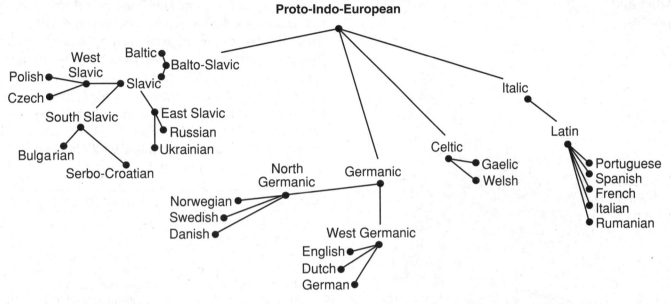

1. Based on the passage and diagram, with which of the following languages does Spanish have the most in common?

   (1) French and Italian
   (2) Swedish and Danish
   (3) Gaelic and Welsh
   (4) English and German
   (5) Russian and Ukrainian

   HINT With which languages does Spanish share a family and common parent language?

2. Why might English and German have become separate languages?

   (1) German is not taught in English schools.
   (2) England is on an island.
   (3) The two languages are in different families.
   (4) German has closer ties to Latin languages.
   (5) German is a Celtic language, English Germanic.

   HINT Which option best provides information that would help you understand the map?

Answers and Explanations

1. (1) French and Italian
Option (1) is correct because the diagram shows French and Italian as belonging to the same language family as Spanish and under a common parent, Latin.

Options (2), (3), (4) and (5) all have different common parents than Spanish (North Germanic, Celtic, West Germanic, and East Slavic, respectively).

2. (2) England is on an island.
Option (2) is correct. The passage notes that barriers such as large bodies of water can lead to language changes; the diagram shows that the two languages once shared a common parent, West Germanic.

Option (1) is not addressed by the passage or diagram. Options (3), (4), and (5) are contradicted by the diagram.

Combine Text and Graphics

Directions: Choose the <u>one best answer</u> to each question.

<u>Question 1</u> refers to the following cartoon and passage.

The term *inflation* refers to a decline in the value of money in relation to the goods and services it will buy.

1. Using the information in the passage, what does the cartoon imply about the economy?

   (1) Available goods, including groceries, have become scarce.
   (2) A good balance exists between prices and available goods.
   (3) The economy is experiencing a high rate of inflation.
   (4) The economy is experiencing a growth spurt.
   (5) Middle-class families have been hardest hit by inflation.

<u>Questions 2 and 3</u> refer to the following passage and chart.

The need for campaign finance reform has been debated in public and in the courts for a number of years. In 1971, the Federal Election Campaign Act was passed to address reform issues. In 1974, the law was amended to continue reform initiatives. In 1976, the constitutionality of the law was tested in the case of *Buckley v. Valeo*. The Supreme Court upheld certain parts of the law while finding other parts unconstitutional.

Constitutional	Unconstitutional
• $2,000 limit on individual contributions	• limit on total contributions
• disclosure of contributors • public financing of elections	• limit on expenditures by candidates from their own personal funds to influence elections

2. The Supreme Court ruled that candidates had a right to spend their own money as they pleased. On which of the following constitutional guarantees did they probably base their opinion?

   (1) freedom of speech
   (2) freedom of the press
   (3) right to trial by jury
   (4) right to privacy
   (5) right to petition the government

3. Which of the following probably reflects the court's thinking on contribution limitations?

   (1) Money should be spent on social issues.
   (2) Money ensures that the right candidate is elected.
   (3) Large contributions may improperly influence an elected official.
   (4) Only the very wealthy can be elected.
   (5) Contributions should be given to charity instead of politics.

Questions 4 through 6 refer to the following passage and map.

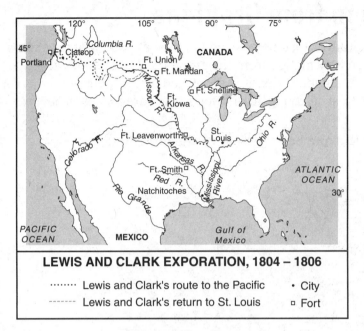

LEWIS AND CLARK EXPORATION, 1804 – 1806

········· Lewis and Clark's route to the Pacific   • City
-------- Lewis and Clark's return to St. Louis   □ Fort

In 1803, after the Louisiana Purchase, President Thomas Jefferson persuaded Congress to appropriate funds for a voyage of discovery to seek out a Northwest Passage. Long dreamed of by explorers and politicians, the Passage, it was hoped, would extend continuously from the Mississippi River to the Pacific Ocean. Meriwether Lewis and William Clark were chosen to lead the expedition. The plan was to begin in St. Louis and travel up the Missouri River, cross the "short portage" from the Missouri to the Columbia River, and thence to the Pacific.

However, the explorers were unable to find a continuous water passage. After torturous false starts and dead ends, coupled with crippling overland journeys, the party finally reached the Columbia River in November 1805. After a winter on the Pacific shore, near present-day Portland, the party began its return trip. In an attempt to find the missing passage, the party split in two. Although the two parties met again on the Missouri, neither had discovered the mythical continuous water route. However, the "Corps of Discovery," as it was called, had managed to map much of the vast lands that became our American West.

4. Based on the map and passage, of what value would a Northwest Passage have been to politicians and business interests?

(1) It might serve to unify the country by connecting the Mississippi to the Pacific.
(2) It would encourage Congress to sell the Louisiana Purchase.
(3) A similar passage might be discovered in the Southeast.
(4) Northeastern fur traders wanted to bring their wares to Portland.
(5) European settlers in Portland wanted to take trips back east.

5. Based on the map and passage, what is the most likely reason St. Louis was chosen as the starting point for the expedition?

(1) It was on the same latitude as Washington, D.C.
(2) It was located near the juncture of the Mississippi and Missouri Rivers.
(3) It was the capital of the Louisiana Purchase.
(4) It was already a great railway center.
(5) It was a center of higher education.

6. What misconception on the part of Lewis and Clark may have contributed to some of the difficulties they encountered?

(1) The Pacific Ocean was much closer.
(2) The Rocky Mountains were smaller.
(3) There was only a short portage between the Missouri and Columbia Rivers.
(4) They could follow an existing map of the Northwest.
(5) Louisiana bordered on the Pacific Ocean.

[**TIP**

When answering a question based on a combined passage and graphic, refer to both sources, not just one or the other.

Answers and explanations start on page 120.

Combine Information from Graphics

Some questions on the GED Social Studies Test may ask you to look at two graphics and answer questions based on combined information from the graphics. You could be asked to summarize information, restate a main idea, identify causes and effects, identify implications, or draw conclusions. When selecting an answer, make sure you consider the information from both graphics.

Look at the photograph. Choose the <u>one best answer</u> to the question.

Composite photograph showing Los Angeles, California, on a clear day (March 2) and on a day with dense smog (March 31).

QUESTION: Which of the following conclusions can be drawn from the photograph?

(1) Smog-causing pollution has been reduced throughout the U.S.
(2) Smog is worse during January and February than it is in March.
(3) The later in the month, the more likely Los Angeles will experience clear days.
(4) The density of smog can differ from day to day.
(5) Smog is prevalent only in large cities such as Los Angeles.

EXPLANATIONS

STEP **1**   To answer this question, ask yourself:

- What are the photographs about? <u>the same area of Los Angeles on a clear day and on a day with dense smog</u>
- What is the question asking me to do? <u>Choose the conclusion that best supports the information shown in the images.</u>

STEP **2**   Evaluate all of the answer choices and choose the <u>best</u> answer.

(1) No. This conclusion is not supported by the composite photograph.
(2) No. Neither the composite photograph nor the caption indicates that smog varies predictably by month of the year.
(3) No. Neither the composite photograph nor the caption indicates that smog varies predictably by days within a given month.
(4) Yes. The smog levels vary on the two different days shown in the composite photograph.
(5) No. Nothing in the composite photograph or caption suggests that only large cities have smog.

ANSWER: (4) The density of smog can differ from day to day.

Practice the Skill

Try these examples. Choose the <u>one best answer</u> to each question. Then check your answers and the explanations.

Population of the Ten Largest American Cities—1880	
New York	1,773,000
Philadelphia	847,000
Chicago	503,000
Boston	363,000
St. Louis	351,000
Baltimore	332,000
Cincinnati	255,000
Pittsburgh	235,000
San Francisco	234,000
New Orleans	216,000

Population of the Ten Largest American Cities—1900	
New York	3,437,000
Chicago	1,699,000
Philadelphia	1,294,000
St. Louis	575,000
Boston	561,000
Baltimore	509,000
Pittsburgh	452,000
Cleveland	382,000
Buffalo	352,000
San Francisco	343,000

1. Which of the following cities was one of the ten largest American cities in both 1880 and 1900?

   (1) Cincinnati
   (2) New Orleans
   (3) Cleveland
   (4) Buffalo
   (5) San Francisco

   HINT Which option restates information from the tables indicating a city that was one of the ten largest in both 1880 and 1900?

2. According to the tables, what happened to the population of Chicago between 1880 and 1900?

   (1) It stayed about the same.
   (2) It doubled in size.
   (3) It more than tripled in size.
   (4) It became larger than New York.
   (5) It became equal to the population of Philadelphia.

   HINT Which option <u>best</u> describes the relation between Chicago's population in 1880 and its population in 1900?

Answers and Explanations

1. (5) San Francisco
According to the tables, San Francisco (option 5) is the only city that was one of the ten largest in 1880 and again in 1900.

Options (1) and (2) are incorrect because Cincinnati and New Orleans were in the top ten in 1880, but not in 1900. Options (3) and (4) are incorrect because Cleveland and Buffalo were in the top ten in 1900, but not in 1880.

2. (3) It more than tripled in size.
Option (3) is correct; Chicago's population went from about 500,000 in 1880 to well over 1.5 million in 1900.

Options (1), (2), (4), and (5) are incorrect and contradicted by information in the tables.

Combine Information from Graphics

Directions: Choose the one best answer to each question.

<u>Questions 1 through 4</u> refer to the following graphs and passage about supply and demand.

Supply Curve

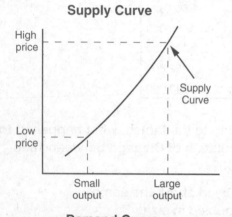

Demand Curve

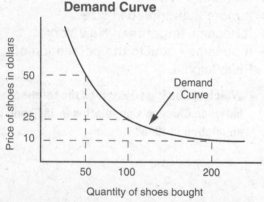

In traditional economics, supply and demand interact to determine prices in the market. Supply refers to the amount of a product a producer will provide at various prices. Demand refers to the quantity of a product consumers want and can buy at various prices.

1. According to the supply curve shown in the graph, what causes output to rise?

   (1) higher prices
   (2) lower prices
   (3) larger output
   (4) smaller output
   (5) lower prices and larger output

2. According to the demand curve shown in the graph, what causes demand to increase?

   (1) higher prices
   (2) greater supply
   (3) decreasing supply
   (4) lower prices
   (5) higher prices and larger supply

3. Based on the principles of supply and demand, what factors might cause a retailer to lower the price of an item?

   (1) small supply and high demand
   (2) small supply alone
   (3) large supply and low demand
   (4) high demand alone
   (5) large supply and high demand

4. Which of the following <u>best</u> states an unstated assumption based on combined information from the graphs?

   (1) The less a product costs, the more of it consumers are likely to buy.
   (2) The more a product costs, the more of it consumers are likely to buy.
   (3) Producers want to make as many products as they can, and to sell those products at the highest possible prices.
   (4) Consumers want to buy as many products as possible at the lowest possible prices.
   (5) Both (3) and (4).

> **TIP**
>
> When answering a question based on multiple graphics, always examine each graphic multiple times before you pick an answer.

Questions 5 and 6 refer to the following flowchart and table.

How a Bill Becomes Law

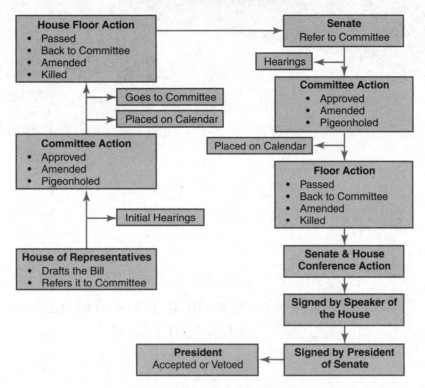

Legislation Fact and Fiction

FACT	FICTION
Anyone can draft a bill, but only members of Congress can introduce legislation.	The president of the United States can introduce legislation.
The legislative process is slow moving, often taking months or years for a bill to make its way through the entire process and be signed into law by the president of the United States.	Throughout the process, there is little chance for the House and Senate to discuss specific parts of the bill.
If a bill can make it through committee action, it has a greater likelihood of making its way through the entire process.	If a bill is killed in floor action, it cannot be rewritten and resubmitted to the legislative process.

5. Which of the following conclusions is best supported by the information in the table and flowchart?

(1) A bill may be drafted by a committee in the House of Representatives.
(2) A bill may be submitted by the president if the House and Senate agree.
(3) A bill does not have to go through the entire legislative process if it is approved in the initial hearings.
(4) The legislative process is complicated and can take a long time to complete.
(5) The legislative process should be changed to reflect current needs of the U.S.

6. A bill can be stopped at many points in the process. At what point is a bill most likely to receive its greatest scrutiny?

(1) during committee action
(2) during floor action
(3) during the conference committee between the House and Senate
(4) when the president approves or vetoes it
(5) when the bill comes up for debate

Answers and explanations start on page 120.

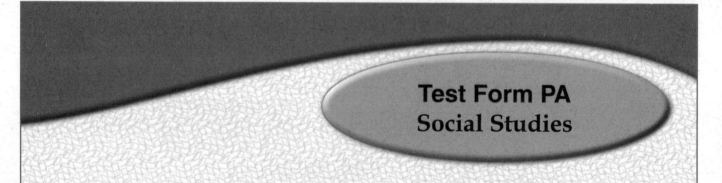

Test Form PA
Social Studies

Tests of
General Educational
Development

Social Studies
Official GED Practice Test

GED Testing Service
American Council on Education

SOCIAL STUDIES
Tests of General Educational Development
Directions

The Social Studies Test consists of multiple-choice questions that measure general social studies concepts. The questions are based on short readings that often include a map, graph, chart, cartoon, or figure. Study the information given and then answer the question(s) following it. Refer to the information as often as necessary in answering the questions.

You will have 35 minutes to answer the 25 questions in this booklet. Work carefully, but do not spend too much time on any one question. Answer every question.

Do not mark in this test booklet. Record your answers on the separate answer sheet provided. Be sure that all requested information is properly recorded on the answer sheet.

To record your answers, fill in the numbered circle on the answer sheet that corresponds to the answer you select for each question in the test booklet.

FOR EXAMPLE:

Early colonists of North America looked for settlement sites with adequate water supplies and access by ship. For this reason, many early towns were built near

(1) mountains
(2) prairies
(3) rivers
(4) glaciers
(5) plateaus

(On Answer Sheet)

The correct answer is "rivers"; therefore, answer space 3 would be marked on the answer sheet.

Do not rest the point of your pencil on the answer sheet while you are considering your answer. Make no stray or unnecessary marks. If you change an answer, erase your first mark completely. Mark only <u>one</u> answer space for each question; multiple answers will be scored as incorrect. Do not fold or crease your answer sheet. All test materials must be returned to the test administrator.

DO NOT BEGIN TAKING THIS TEST UNTIL TOLD TO DO SO

Component: 9993949124
Kit: **ISBN 0-7398-5433-X**

4   **Social Studies**

Directions: Choose the <u>one best answer</u> to each question.

<u>Questions 1 and 2</u> refer to the following world map.

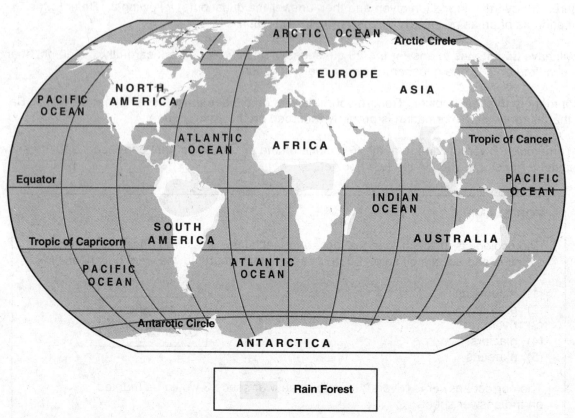

World's Rain Forests in 1999

Source: Adapted from "Taking Care of Our Earth," *Wenatchee (Wash.) World*, 1 March 1999, 8.

1. What will most likely happen if the ecology in the ecosystem featured in the map continues to be destroyed?

    (1) The biodiversity of the areas will be lost.
    (2) The price of beef products will fall.
    (3) New plants will be discovered as the land is logged.
    (4) More people will be able to harvest the vegetation there.
    (5) Ecotourism will increase in these areas.

2. What factors of physical or cultural geography directly determine the location of the ecosystems featured in the map?

    (1) mountainous terrain and moderate precipitation
    (2) growing population and industry in urban centers
    (3) year-round rainfall and warm temperatures
    (4) human agricultural settlement and trade patterns
    (5) middle latitudes and cold ocean currents

GO ON TO THE NEXT PAGE

3. The United States generates 4.5 billion pounds of toxic waste each year. Much toxic waste is composed of cancer-causing chemical compounds that remain after the production of chemicals, paper, metals, and plastics.

    Based on this information, what does improper disposal of toxic waste in the United States most likely produce?

    (1) poisoned water supply
    (2) a fuel crisis
    (3) decrease in illnesses
    (4) fertile soil
    (5) recycled materials

4. Some large companies use vocational retraining programs to teach people to do work that is different from their present jobs. The retraining is often necessary because some employees' jobs are no longer needed to make a company's product.

    What is the main purpose of these programs?

    (1) to encourage people to leave the company
    (2) to improve the quality of products
    (3) to increase the salaries of employees
    (4) to make it possible for people to continue to work
    (5) to promote people to higher-paying jobs

Question 5 refers to the following photograph.

"Why, good afternoon. Yes, it is a shame. He should have fixed it before we came."
Photograph for advertisement by Gerald Carson, ca. 1913.
Courtesy of Culver Pictures.

5. What irony about the history of transportation has the photographer depicted in this photograph?

    (1) Horse-drawn vehicles were initially more dependable than internal combustion engines.
    (2) The automobile was faster than the horse.
    (3) The internal combustion engine never became cost-effective.
    (4) Automobiles were luxuries that few people could afford at the time.
    (5) Long-distance road travel was common at the time.

GO ON TO THE NEXT PAGE

6   Social Studies

Question 6 refers to the following diagram.

News Media Usage by Americans

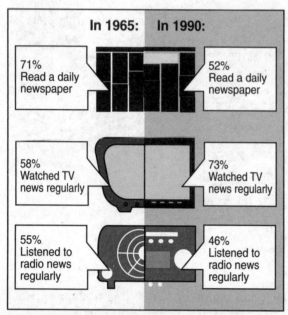

In 1965:   In 1990:

71% Read a daily newspaper

52% Read a daily newspaper

58% Watched TV news regularly

73% Watched TV news regularly

55% Listened to radio news regularly

46% Listened to radio news regularly

Source: Adapted from Gary B. Nash, *American Odyssey: The United States in the Twentieth Century* (Lake Forest, Ill.: Glencoe/Macmillan/McGraw-Hill, 1997), 726.

6. Through which medium would the government in 1990 have been likely to attract the attention of most of the electorate to a political issue?

    (1) newspapers
    (2) magazines
    (3) television
    (4) radio
    (5) live theatre

Question 7 refers to the following cartoon.

7. In the United States mail service is available to all people.

    What does this cartoon imply about its future use?

    (1) The mail is likely to be censored by the federal government.
    (2) The computerized postal service will discourage free speech among citizens.
    (3) Electronic mail will violate the U.S. Constitution.
    (4) Technological changes will alter the way citizens communicate by mail.
    (5) Inflation is a constant problem for the U.S. government in its efforts to provide services to its citizens.

GO ON TO THE NEXT PAGE

Questions 8 and 9 refer to the following information.

Based on Standard U.S. Government Tests

ENERGYGUIDE

Clothes Washer
Capacity Standard
Top Loading

Model(s) MAV5000

Compare the Energy Use of this Clothes Washer with Others before You Buy.

This Model Uses
897 kWh/year*

Energy use (kWh/year) range of all similar models

Uses Least Energy	Uses Most Energy
294	1231

*kWh/year (kilowatt-hours per year) is a measure of energy (electricity) use. Your utility company uses it to compute your bill. Only standard size, top loading clothes washers are used in this scale.

Clothes washers using more energy cost more to operate. This model's estimated yearly operating cost is

$76   **$29**

When used with an electric water heater

When used with a natural gas water heater

Based on eight loads of clothes a week and a 1998 U.S. government national average cost of 8.42¢ per kWh for electricity and 61.9¢ per therm for natural gas. Your actual operating cost will vary depending on your local utility rates and your use of the product.

Canada

Energy consumption/
Consommation énergétique

897 kWh
per year / par année

This model /Ce modèle ▼

259 kWh	984 kWh
Uses least energy / Consomme le moins d'énergie	Uses most energy / Consomme le plus d'énergie

Standard/Ordinaire

Similar models compared	Modèles similaires comparés
number MAV5000 SERIES	Numéro du modèle

8. How are these guides useful to U.S. and Canadian consumers?

The guides

(1) are too general to be of much practical use
(2) can give information for comparison shopping
(3) quickly go out of date as fuel prices change
(4) show how to assemble the appliance
(5) show consumers how to use the appliance

9. Which of the following best explains why the U.S. and Canadian governments would support the use of the guides?

(1) to encourage the conservation of national energy resources
(2) to increase government regulations
(3) to monitor consumer spending habits
(4) to ensure that consumers buy clothes washers
(5) to discourage competitive prices among manufacturers

GO ON TO THE NEXT PAGE

8   Social Studies

Questions 10 through 13 refer to the following information.

By the early 1800s, the Cherokees had been pushed into a small section of the southern Appalachians. They had established farms and small manufacturing shops, built schools, and published a newspaper in their own language. They governed themselves under a written constitution with a legislature, courts, and militia. The Cherokees, while adapting to white culture in some instances, valued their own traditions and formed a separate state on their lands. The Georgia legislature refused to recognize the Cherokee state and opened all Cherokee land to white settlement.

In 1831, the U.S. Supreme Court, led by Chief Justice John Marshall, ruled that the Cherokee Nation had clearly defined boundaries within which "the laws of Georgia can have no force." The Court further ruled that Georgia citizens could not enter Cherokee territory without Cherokee consent.

However, President Andrew Jackson rejected the Supreme Court decision. Against the strong protests of several members of Congress, he allowed illegal seizures of Cherokee lands to continue, and in 1838, the Cherokees were forced to move to unsettled lands west of the Mississippi. During their 800-mile journey, made mostly on foot, thousands of Cherokees died on the "Trail of Tears."

In 1890, a member of the U.S. Cavalry wrote: "The long, painful journey to the West ended on March 26, 1839, with 4000 silent graves reaching from the foothills of the Smoky Mountains to what is known as Indian territory in the West. And covetousness [greed] on the part of the white race was the cause of all that the Cherokee had to suffer. . . ."

John Ehle, adapted from *Trail of Tears, Rise and Fall of the Cherokee Nation*, Archer Books, 1988, 394.

10. What happened as the Cherokees adopted many U.S. customs and institutions in the early 1800s?

    The Cherokees

    (1) were accepted by white society
    (2) gave up their Cherokee arts and traditions
    (3) bought more lands west of the Mississippi
    (4) were recognized as citizens of Georgia
    (5) decided to become an independent state

11. Which best describes the way President Jackson responded to the 1831 Supreme Court decision about Cherokee territory?

    President Jackson

    (1) disregarded constitutional law
    (2) enforced separation of powers
    (3) played party politics
    (4) enforced judicial review
    (5) supported political democracy for all

12. What is the basis for the U.S. Cavalry officer's evaluation of the Cherokee experience on the "Trail of Tears"?

    (1) his loyalty as a member of the Cherokees
    (2) his pride in the U.S. military
    (3) his support for the government's actions
    (4) his recognition of an injustice
    (5) his acceptance of society's ways

GO ON TO THE NEXT PAGE

13. "It is presumed that humanity dictated the original policy of the removal and concentration of the Indians in the West to save them from extinction. But today, by reason of the immense growth of the American population, . . . the Indian races are more seriously threatened with a speedy extermination than ever before. . . ."

Donehogawa, first Native American Commissioner of Indian Affairs, 1870.

Donehogawa's 1870 statement supports which conclusion regarding the history of the Cherokee people?

(1) The Cherokee culture and economy were similar to those of most other Native American groups.
(2) Andrew Jackson's decisions protected the Cherokee people from danger.
(3) Cherokee conflicts with the U.S. policies were similar to the experience of other Native American groups.
(4) Other Native American nations shared their desire for U.S. statehood.
(5) The U.S. government supported the desire of the Cherokees to keep their land and laws.

14. Many wine tasters are trained to judge the quality of wines. By tasting a particular wine, they can identify the region and country from which the wine comes. The taste is influenced by the type of soil in which the wine grapes grow.

These facts best support which generalization about wine production?

(1) Heat and light are not important in wine production.
(2) The quality of wine grapes does not vary.
(3) Chemicals in nature generally harm wine production.
(4) Wine production is affected more by human intervention than by nature.
(5) Geographic conditions affect wine production.

Question 15 refers to the following graph.

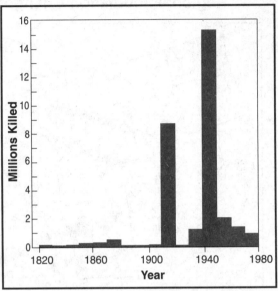

Deaths from International Wars, 1820–1980

Sources: J. David Singer and Melvin Small, adapted from *The Wages of War, 1815-1965: A Statistical Handbook* (New York: John Wiley, 1972); and Small and Singer, *Resort to Arms* (Beverly Hills, Calif.: Sage, 1982).

15. Which question about the history of international wars can be answered by using information in the graph?

(1) Why did the number of deaths caused by war increase in the twentieth century?
(2) During which decade in the twentieth century did war cause the most deaths?
(3) To what extent did the number of war deaths change in 1990?
(4) How many civilians, compared with soldiers, died in international wars?
(5) Which areas of the world have been most severely affected by war?

GO ON TO THE NEXT PAGE

10   Social Studies

Question 16 refers to the following map.

Regional Population Changes in the United States, 1940–1950

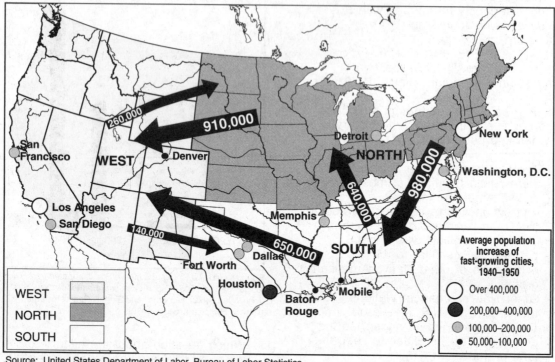

Source: United States Department of Labor, Bureau of Labor Statistics.

16. Which conclusion about migration during
World War II is confirmed by clear
evidence in the map?

   (1) Fewer people migrated during this
   time than before World War II.
   (2) The majority of migrants were women
   workers.
   (3) The government encouraged people
   to move to the North.
   (4) Racial tensions developed in several
   cities.
   (5) A large number of people moved to
   the West.

GO ON TO THE NEXT PAGE

Questions 17 through 19 refer to the following information.

The governments of Canada and the United States are federal systems (that is, power is divided between the national government and smaller, subnational governments). In the United States, power is divided between the central government and fifty states. In Canada, separate powers are assigned to the national government and to the governments of the ten provinces and the territories. In both countries some powers, such as the right to coin money or manage foreign affairs, may be exercised only by the national government. By contrast, states and provinces exercise important powers over education and local property.

Under federalism, the central and subnational governments also share many powers. In Canada and the United States, the national government works with the provinces or states to combat crime, clean the environment, and provide for the needy. Although the United States and Canada rank among the world's most affluent nations, their citizens include the disabled, the unemployed, and single parents who cannot earn enough to provide for their children.

In the United States, a needy single parent may receive payments from federal and state governments, medical care funded by both levels of government, and food stamps financed by the national government. In Canada, the national and provincial governments contribute to some health care for all citizens. Needy single parents may obtain food and shelter benefits by applying through local and provincial governments.

Since welfare benefits are financed partially by state or provincial governments, they may vary according to where one lives. The welfare check of a single parent in Nova Scotia may be very different from that of a single parent in Alberta. Similarly, U.S. welfare benefits differ greatly from Maine to California.

17. Which of the following is a federal system of government?

(1) In New Zealand, power is exercised by a popularly elected parliament.
(2) In Saudi Arabia, the king holds all executive and legislative powers.
(3) In France, the constitution provides that all major powers are exercised by the National Assembly and Ministries in Paris.
(4) In England, all important powers are vested in the national parliament in London.
(5) In Mexico, power is divided between the national government and the governments of thirty-one states.

18. Which of the following is a reason for adopting a federal system of government?

(1) Power would be concentrated in the hands of a few people at the national level.
(2) Governments would have very little influence in peoples' lives.
(3) Governments would respond differently to national and local issues.
(4) Fewer elected officials would be needed.
(5) Local governments would give up all of their power.

19. Which of the following comparisons between the United States and Canada is supported by the information?

(1) The national government in Canada is more powerful than the national government in the United States.
(2) Both U.S. and Canadian national and subnational governments provide benefits to needy citizens.
(3) States in the United States are larger than provinces in Canada.
(4) A greater number of poor people live in Canada than in the United States.
(5) Both the U.S. and Canadian national governments pay for unlimited amounts of health care for their citizens.

GO ON TO THE NEXT PAGE

12   **Social Studies**

Questions 20 through 23 refer to the following time line and viewpoint.

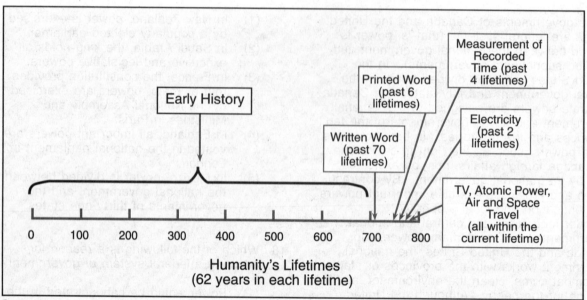

Source: Adapted from Alvin Toffler, 1970.

Alvin Toffler, a famous "futurist," developed the above time line in 1970. He divided the past 50,000 years of history into lifetimes of 62 years each. According to Toffler's "800 lifetimes," many of humanity's major technological benefits have been developed within a few "lifetimes."

The quality of many people's lives depends on how technology is used. But the challenge to society is how skillfully people can adapt to such great changes in technology, lifestyles, and environment. In 1970, Charles Reich warned people of the dangers of uncontrolled technology when he wrote:

"Technology and production can be benefactors of man, but they are mindless instruments. If undirected, they career along with a momentum of their own. . . .

"Organizations and bureaucracy, which are applications of technology to social institutions, increasingly dictate how we shall live our lives, with the logic of organizations taking precedence over any other value."

Source: James O. Lugo, adapted from *Living Psychology*, 4th ed. (CAT Publishing Company, Calif., 1991), 349–51.

20. According to the time line, which of the following statements most accurately describes the historical development of technological changes?

 (1) Technological changes have developed at a steady pace.
 (2) Every human "lifetime" has produced major technological changes.
 (3) Most important technological changes occurred during the same ten-year period.
 (4) Technological change has slowed down in the past 100 years.
 (5) Technological changes have happened more frequently in the past two lifetimes than before.

21. What would Charles Reich have called the nuclear weapons that proliferated during the twentieth century?

 (1) a bureaucracy
 (2) mindless instruments
 (3) logical organization
 (4) social institutions
 (5) controlled technology

GO ON TO THE NEXT PAGE

22. Which of the following is an example of people adapting to the new technology of the latest lifetime shown in the time line?

    People

    (1) are less likely to travel
    (2) read books from other countries
    (3) adjust their activities to seasonal changes
    (4) exchange information rapidly
    (5) grow their own food

23. How does the passage defend the idea that technological developments challenge people in their daily lives in the twentieth century?

    By claiming that

    (1) technology was expensive
    (2) people did not want to belong to organizations
    (3) many societies did not have modern technology
    (4) people needed skills that helped them live with new technology
    (5) technological changes took too long to occur for people to benefit from them

24. Which of the following is the most reasonable explanation for a surplus of a product on the market?

    (1) Most consumers find the product reasonably priced.
    (2) The producers overestimated the demand for the product.
    (3) An expensive substitute for the product is available.
    (4) Producers have not supplied enough of the product.
    (5) The product has many uses.

Question 25 refers to the following information.

In 1990, the U.S. Environmental Protection Agency (EPA) published a report that identified four "relatively high-risk" environmental problems that would be given priority in the coming years. All of them were global in scope: climate change, ozone depletion, destruction and change of wildlife habitat, and species extinction.

The EPA reported that it is likely to devote an increasing proportion of its resources to life on Earth and relatively less to reestablish, for example, the dioxin-tainted town of Times Beach, Missouri. The inhabitants of Earth, unlike the town, have nowhere else to go.

25. On the basis of this information, which best explains the EPA's reasoning?

    (1) Local environmental problems must be solved first.
    (2) Studies are needed more than actions to solve global environmental problems.
    (3) Global environmental problems must be solved or Earth will be uninhabitable.
    (4) Each local community should solve its own environmental problems.
    (5) Immediate answers to environmental problems are likely.

END OF EXAMINATION

To determine the standard score for the *Official GED Practice Test Form PA: Social Studies:*
1. Locate the number of questions the candidate answered correctly on the multiple-choice test.
2. Read the corresponding standard score from the column on the right.

Compare the candidate's standard scores to the minimum score requirements in the jurisdiction in which the GED credential is to be issued. (See *Appendix D* in the *Official GED Practice Tests Administrator's Manual*.)

U.S. Edition Form PA Social Studies	
Number of Correct Answers	Estimated GED Test Standard Score
25	800
24	700
23	630
22	580
21	550
20	530
19	500
18	490
17	470
16	450
15	440
14	430
13	410
12	400
11	380
10	370
9	350
8	340
7	320
6	300
5	280
4	260
3	230
2	210
1	200

Social Studies Answers

1. 1
2. 3
3. 1
4. 4
5. 1
6. 3
7. 4
8. 2
9. 1
10. 5
11. 1
12. 4
13. 3
14. 5
15. 2
16. 5
17. 5
18. 3
19. 2
20. 5
21. 2
22. 4
23. 4
24. 2
25. 3

Pretest Answers and Explanations

1. **(4) Nunavut** Option (4) is correct because according to the table, it has an area of 818,959 square miles, which is the greatest number. Prince Edward Island (option 1) is incorrect because it had the smallest area. Ontario (option 2) is incorrect because while it has the greatest population—10,753,573—its area was about 400,000 fewer square miles than Nunavut. Quebec (option 3) was not correct; although it has very large numbers in both columns, its area was less than that of Nunavut. The Northwest Territories (option 5) is incorrect because its area is 503,951 square miles, which is less than that of Nunavut.

2. **(1) Canada has a wide diversity of population densities.** Option (1) is correct because it can be inferred from the table that the population densities in each province are not the same. This answer requires an understanding of the information presented in the table. Population density is the number of people in a given area. Option (2) is false because according to the table, Quebec is the second biggest province in Canada, not the biggest. Option (3) contradicts information in the table because the biggest province, Nunavut, actually has the smallest population. Option (4) is not correct because the most populous province, Ontario, is actually the fourth largest province, not the largest. There are five provinces, not only two, with populations over 1 million, so option (5) is incorrect.

3. **(5) The Crusaders traveled from west to east.** Option (5) best matches the information shown on the map, which indicates that the *general* route had an eastern direction. While the map indicates the Crusaders' route went through Constantinople (option 1), that the Fourth Crusade traveled by sea from Venice to Constantinople (option 3), and that Crusaders embarked from Vézelay, Venice, and Regensburg (option 4), none of these statements is the best description of the Crusaders' general route. While it is true that the First Crusade temporarily occupied four Crusader States (Antioch, Tripoli, Acre, and Jerusalem), option (2) is incorrect because the information is provided only by the passage and cannot be determined from the map.

4. **(2) The Crusaders were unable to save Jerusalem from the "infidels."** Option (2) gives the best brief description of the ideas included in the passage, which indicates the Crusades were primarily an attempt to capture and "save" Jerusalem, which ended with the Turkish capture of Constantinople and founding of the Ottoman Empire. The statement that Jerusalem was made permanently a Crusader State by the First Crusade (option 1) is contradicted by the text, which notes the capture of Jerusalem by Crusaders was temporary. The passage does not provide information or make suggestions about papal support for the Crusades (option 3). While it is true Constantinople was conquered in 1453 (option 4), this is a detail, not the main idea of the passage. Nothing in the passage suggests that the Crusades consolidated the Holy Roman Empire (option 5).

5. **(3) Tripoli** Option (3) is correct. According to the passage and map, Tripoli was one of four temporarily occupied Crusader States from Antioch south to Jerusalem. Nothing in the passage or map suggests that Rome (option 1), Edessa (option 2), Constantinople (option 4), or Venice (option 5) were Crusader States.

6. **(3) Honor and pride were highly valued in Japan.** Option (3) is correct and supported by the passage's emphasis on the samurai's honor, pride, and effectiveness. While it is true that the samurai were fierce warriors (option 1), this is a detail of the passage, not an inference based on the passage. Nothing in the passage suggests that the Japanese people who were not samurai were materialistic (option 2), that Japanese culture collapsed in 1876 with the abolishment of the samurai lifestyle (option 4), or that seppuku was an expression of religious faith (option 5).

7. **(1) respects the samurai** Option (1) is correct and is supported by the writer's highly positive description of samurai. Option (2)—that the writer dislikes the samurai—is incorrect and contradicted by details in the passage indicating the opposite. The statements that the writer doesn't care about the samurai (option 3) or isn't sure what he or she thinks about them (option 4) are not supported by the passage. Nothing in the passage suggests that the writer is wary, or afraid, of the samurai (option 5).

8. **(4) As a percentage of total population, there were more foreign-born residents in the U.S. in 1910 than at any other time since 1850.** Option (4) correctly restates information from the bar graph, which shows foreign-born populations in the U.S. as a percentage of total population. The statements that birth rates for immigrants are steadily increasing (option 1) or falling (option 5) are incorrect because the bar graph does not provide information about birth rates. Option (2) is an opinion about acceptance of immigrants that is not supported by the graph, which shows only facts. The statement that there were more foreign-born residents in the U.S. in 1910 than at any time since 1850 (option 3) is incorrect because the graph does not give total population numbers but rather shows foreign-born residents as a percentage of total population.

9. **(1) The U.S. government has laws to prevent monopolies.** Option (1) correctly states a fact based on the passage, which indicates Congress has passed several laws to discourage monopolies and promote competition. The statements that big business is bad for the economy (option 2) and that the U.S. government must regulate business to stop exploitation (option 3) are opinions, not facts based on the passage. The passage does not address the effectiveness of the Sherman and Clayton Acts (option 4), nor does it state that monopolies are no longer a problem in the United States (option 5).

10. **(5) The U.S. Congress discourages monopolies and encourages competitive pricing.** Option (5) is the best restatement of information in the passage describing efforts by Congress to curb monopolies and maintain competition. Option (2) is opposite the correct answer; monopolies don't encourage competition—rather, they discourage it. Option (3) is incorrect because the passage describes the stance of Congress in regard to monopolies as an oppositional force proactive in discouraging them. The statement that monopolies lead to better products or services, despite high prices (option 4), is not supported by information in the passage.

11. **(5) Consumers can't always protect themselves.** Option (5) is correct. In passing laws to protect consumers, the government is assuming that consumers need

protection. Options (1) and (4) are incorrect because they assume the opposite—that consumers don't need protection. Options (2) and (3)—that consumers dislike government intervention or are basically ignorant about what they are purchasing—are assumptions that are not addressed in or supported by the passage.

12. **(3) The U.S. Consumer Product Safety Commission works with foreign manufacturers to make sure they understand the regulations and safety concerns of importing toys into the U.S.** Option (3) is correct. As the passage indicates, the purpose of consumer protection laws is to set standards for safety on products such as automobiles, children's clothing, toys, and other products. Option (1) is incorrect; nothing in the passage suggests *Unsafe at Any Speed* was a result of the consumer protection laws. While a fifteen-passenger van may indeed be safer than a compact (option 2) and a government watchdog agency did report that 20 percent of the toys made and sold in China pose safety risks (option 4), nothing in the passage supports these ideas as results of the consumer protection laws. While it is true that the U.S. Environmental Protection Agency has programs to protect the nation's water (option 5), the agency's mission is protection of human health and the environment, not consumer protection.

13. **(1) Many women must pay for their family's everyday needs.** Option (1) is correct. The graph shows that nearly one-third of the women with two jobs are working a second job in order to meet and pay for household expenses, which are a part of a family's everyday needs. There is nothing in the graph to suggest that either option (2) or option (3) is true. Options (4) and (5) are reasons stated on the graph, but they represent smaller portions of the graph, which means they are not the most likely reasons.

14. **(3) Some homeowners disagree with eminent domain and will fight to resist government's attempts to take their homes.** Option (3) is the best option because the cartoon shows a homeowner who is resisting eminent domain to the bitter end. Option (1) is incorrect because the homeowner is visibly upset about the new construction taking place around him. Option (2) is incorrect because it contradicts the cartoon, which seems to indicate that many homeowners do not support eminent domain. The statement that eminent domain is unconstitutional (option 4) is not true and not implied by the cartoon. The statement that eminent domain is unfair to homeowners (option 5) is not an implication suggested by the cartoon.

15. **(5) None of the above.** Option (5) is the correct option because none of the options identify causes that can be determined from information on the graph, which shows percentage of the population that is obese as it increases over time. Option (1) is a possible cause that is not supported by the graph, which does not show how many Americans eat fast food or junk food or how often they do so. The statement that Americans spent almost twice as much time in their cars in 2007 than they did before 1990 (option 2) is not supported by the graph, which doesn't indicate the amount of time people spend in cars. While it's true that the majority of the population is not obese (option 3) and that the rise in percentage of population that is obese was highest in 1997–1998 (option 4), these are details of the graph, not causes for the increase.

16. **(3) Obesity rates have climbed, while smoking rates have declined.** Option (3) offers the best brief description of the main points of the graphs, one of which shows climbing obesity rates, the other declining smoking rates. Options (1) and (2) are incorrect because, as the smoking rates graph indicates, smoking declined during the period in question. Option (4) is an opinion that is not true and is not supported by the information in the graphs, which does not show a relationship between obesity and smoking. Option (5) is incorrect because while declining smoking rates and rising obesity rates would seem to point to lower general fitness, the graph does not address fitness, and nothing in the graphs indicates that Americans do not smoke anymore.

17. **(3) Both protestors and police are content to avoid violent confrontation.** Option (3) is the best generalization that can be made. It is supported both by the photograph, which shows demonstrators and police showing mutual respect, and by the passage, which says violence saddened both anti-war protestors and their adversaries. While the passage indicates that the Kent State shootings saddened people on both sides of the anti-war divide (option 1), this is not the best answer because it is not the primary generalization to be made from the photograph and passage. Nothing in the photograph and passage suggests that violent protest is always preferable to peaceful protest (option 2). Nothing in the passage or photograph supports the generalization that demonstrations held on sunny days tend to be violence free (option 4) or that the demonstrators at Kent State crossed a line that resulted in their being fired upon (option 5).

18. **(5) This is a peaceful protest, with protestors and authorities each calmly holding their ground.** Option (5) is the best implication from the photo based on the relative positions and body language of the participants. While the presence of military police (option 1) implies that there is a protest, disagreement, or confrontation that requires authority control, the mere presence of police does not imply that the confrontation is violent. Option (2) is incorrect because nothing in the photograph implies that the girl is angry at or taunting the police. Whether or not anyone knows what to do next (option 3), this option is incorrect because it is not an implication about whether the confrontation is violent or peaceful. While it is true that the flower is offered by the girl as a symbolic gesture of peace (option 4), this is a detail of the photograph, not its primary implication.

19. **(3) He was not informed of his rights.** Option (5) is correct. As the passage notes, Miranda was questioned and confessed before police informed him of his rights. For this reason, the Supreme Court determined that his confession could not be held against him. Nothing in the passage suggests that Miranda was the victim of police brutality (option 1) or that he was not guilty of committing the accused crimes (option 2). Option (4) is contradicted by the passage, which states that Miranda did not remain silent in

police custody but confessed before he was told that he had the right to see a lawyer. Option (5) is incorrect. The passage doesn't say that Miranda never had a lawyer, only that he was not told of his right to one in a timely fashion.

20. **(5) Geraldine Ferraro was the first woman candidate for Vice President of the United States.** Option (5) best restates the information from the timeline for 1984. Option (1) is incorrect and contradicted by the timeline, which shows Jeannette Rankin of Montana was elected to the U.S. House of Representatives in 1916—four years prior to the ratification of the 19th Amendment. Option (2) is incorrect. The timeline shows Ferraro was the first candidate for vice president of the United States, not president. Option (3) is incorrect. Robinson was elected president of Ireland in 1990, not 1980. Option (4) is incorrect because while it is true that California elected two women senators in 1992, the timeline doesn't indicate whether this was the first time this happened.

Answers and Explanations

Skill 1 Restate Information
Pages 12–13

1. (3) 70 percent of the people Option (3) is the correct restatement of data on the graph because approximately 70 percent of the rural population on the vertical axis aligns with the 1880 point on the timeline. Option (1) indicates population density by square mile, which is not the information provided on the graph. Option (2) is a ratio that is inaccurate based on the graph. Options (4) and (5) are incorrect because they indicate numbers of people rather than percentages of total population, and the label on the vertical axis states that the numbers are percentages.

2. (4) 1920 Option (4) is correct because 1920 is the point on the timeline when falling rural population and rising urban population intersect at 50 percent, or half. Per the graph, about 5 percent of population was urban in 1790 (option 1), 10 percent was urban in 1840 (option 2), and 25 percent was urban in 1880 (option 3). By 1970 (option 5), more than 70 percent of population was urban.

3. (2) Between 1883 and 1954, there were no major legal advances in civil rights. Option (2) is correct because, according to the passage, after the 1883 Civil Rights Act reversal, there were no major legal advances until *Brown vs. the Board of Education* in 1954. Option (1) is incorrect because the text does not indicate *Brown vs. the Board of Education* was the last advance in civil rights. Option (3) is incorrect; *Brown vs. the Board of Education* outlawed discrimination in schools, not other places like businesses. Option (4) is not the best answer; the text does not mention African Americans no longer fighting for other civil rights, and it is not logical to assume they would have done so. The text does not mention marches (option 5).

4. (5) the end of "separate but equal" education Option (5) is correct because, according to the passage, after *Brown vs. the Board of Education* "separate but equal" education was finally outlawed. Racial profiling (option 1) is a continuing struggle. Freedom from slavery (option 2) would have accompanied the rights of citizenship and limited equality gained in 1866. For the same reason, option (3) is incorrect; American citizenship was gained not in the civil rights reforms of the 1950s and 1960s but in 1866 with the passing of the Fourteenth Amendment. The right to own property (option 4) is not mentioned in the text.

5. (2) The shapes of the continents have developed gradually during Earth's history. Option (2) is correct because it is a restatement of the passage, which says the continents' shapes have evolved over hundreds of millions of years. Option (1) has nothing to do with the map or passage. Option (3) is incorrect because the passage says the continents may once have fit together in a single mass, but in the future will continue to drift apart. Option (4) is incorrect. Earth's surface is changing only slowly, and a map shows a single view at a single point in time. The ratio of ocean to landmass has not changed (option 5); the landmass has just shifted.

6. (3) All of Earth's land was once clustered together. Option (3) is correct because the top map shows a single large landmass surrounded by water. Option (1) is incorrect because, as the maps suggest, the continents' present day locations are not the same as they were 200 million years ago. According to the labels on the maps, the drift has not occurred rapidly (option 2) but over a long period of time. While the maps might seem to suggest that the ocean is pushing the continents apart (option 4), the phenomenon of continental drift better explains the continents' changed locations. The clarity of borders (option 5) is not an idea addressed.

7. (1) computer-related and health care industries Option (1) is correct because as the chart shows, the four fastest-growing jobs relate to computer technology and health. While veterinary medicine (option 2) is reflected in the chart, these jobs are ranked lower than the computer and health jobs indicated. Jobs in the southwestern U.S. (option 3) and in India and China (option 5) are not covered by the chart. The Bureau of Labor Statistics (option 4) is the source and does not reflect information about fastest-growing jobs.

Skill 2 Summarize Ideas Pages 16–17

1. (5) The Supreme Court was overworked. Option (5) states the main idea from the passage about easing the Supreme Court's burden. This option also summarizes the visual information provided in the cartoon, where the court cases pile up. Nothing in the passage suggests the number before the war was very few (option 1). That the justices were men (option 2) is reflected by the cartoon but is not addressed in the passage. Option (3) is a summary of only the last sentence. That people looked to the Supreme Court to solve their problems (option 4) is not the main idea of the passage or the cartoon.

2. (5) The church controlled many aspects of everyday life. Option (5) is correct because, as the passage states, the church was the dominant force in the region and controlled key aspects of everyday life. That everyone in medieval Europe believed in God (option 1) is not stated or implied in the passage. The passage makes no mention or suggestions of which towns had churches (option 2) or of feudal lords (option 3). Option (4) is a detail of the passage, not a summary.

3. (1) The church was the most powerful force in medieval Europe. Option (1) is correct because the passage states that the church was the dominant force in the region at the time and then includes supporting details. While option (2) may be true, it is only a detail, not the main idea of the passage. Option (3) is the main idea of the second paragraph but not the main idea for the full passage. The passage makes no mention of whether all people of Western Europe were extremely pious (option 4). Option (5) is implied but is not stated in the passage.

4. (1) Seating arrangements on the Supreme Court follow a formal pattern based on length of time

of service on the Court. The main idea of the passage is that there is a pattern to the seating based on seniority. While it is true that seating on the Court could be considered very complex (option 2) and Chief Justice Roberts is head of the Court (option 3), there is more to the main idea of the passage. The passage does not indicate how often those who serve on the Court change (option 4) or how often seating order changes (option 5).

5. **(3) Justice Alito** As the most junior Associate Justice on the Court, Samuel A. Alito, Jr., sits the farthest to the left of Chief Justice Roberts. The Associate Justices mentioned in options (1), (2), (4), and (5) are all more senior than Associate Justice Alito and would therefore be seated in closer positions when the court hears a case.

6. **(3) maritime technology** As the fourth paragraph indicates, option (3) is correct because the seagoing technology of the Vikings was important to later generations in Europe. The Vikings' raids throughout Europe (option 1) would not be a benefit of their influence. Overcrowding (option 2) may have been a cause but was not a benefit. Trade (option 4) and cultural diversity (option 5) might have been affected but are not the main point of the passage.

7. **(2) Ships were crucial to Viking success.** Option (2) is correct because the paragraph states that Vikings' travel and exploration would not have been possible without their technologically advanced ships. Option (1) is incorrect because the paragraph states the Vikings excelled at sea travel, not overland travel. Whether the Vikings loved to travel (option 3) is not addressed in the paragraph. While it is true that the Vikings could travel to Iceland in a week (option 4), this is only a detail of the paragraph. Theories of why the Viking raids began (option 5) are the subject of paragraph 2, not paragraph 3.

KEY Skill 3 Identify Implications
Pages 20–21

1. **(1) The population of the largest sunbelt cities grew, with Phoenix showing the largest increase.** Option (1) is correct because the graph shows positive percentage growth for all six sunbelt cities, with Phoenix having the most growth. Option (2) is contradicted by the graph, which shows the sunbelt cities growing at varying rates. Option (3) is incorrect because the graph does not show population shifts from Houston to San Diego. The graph does not show the relative populations of San Diego and Los Angeles (option 4) or suggest the reasons people might want to move to warm climates (option 5).

2. **(3) Sunbelt cities experienced overall growth in the 1990s, while snowbelt cities experienced an overall drop in population.** Option (3) is correct. Comparing the percentages of total population change in sunbelt cities to that in snowbelt cities reveals that sunbelt cities had an overall growth, while snowbelt cities had an overall drop. While it is true that each type of city—sunbelt and snowbelt—experienced growth at times during the 1990s (option 1), this is not a primary implication of the graph. Option (2) is incorrect; the six sunbelt cities on the graph all experienced positive growth. The six sunbelt cities did not experience similar amounts of growth (option 4). Snowbelt

cities' growth in the 1980s (option 5) is not addressed by the graph.

3. **(3) Population growth in the six largest sunbelt cities was a trend in the 1990s.** That population growth was a trend in the 1990s (option 3) is implied by the graph's indication of positive growth among all six largest sunbelt cities. Option (1) is not implied by and contradicts the graph, which shows the populations of only three of the snowbelt cities declined. The graph does not imply that any city is more popular than any other (option 2). Option (4) is incorrect because the graph does not suggest implications about housing affordability. Option (5) is incorrect because there is no implication from the graph that population shifted from Detroit to Indianapolis.

4. **(2) It can increase and decrease.** Option (2) is a correct implication because as the graph shows, while population in most urban areas increased, it declined in Baltimore, Detroit, and Philadelphia. Option (1) is not implied and is contradicted by the graph, which shows numerous changes in population growth for the six largest sunbelt and snowbelt urban areas. That population in urban areas is declining (option 3) is not implied by and contradicts the graph, which shows population is both rising and declining in urban areas. Option (4) is incorrect. The graph shows population changes for urban areas, but it does not show or imply population shifts from urban to suburban. Option (5) is incorrect. The graph does not show or imply growth of urban areas in the time frame compared to urban growth during other time frames.

5. **(3) The Guptas valued learning.** Though never stated directly, the passage's explanation of the Guptas' intellectual pursuits implies that learning was very important to them (option 3). The passage does not address or make implications about the geographic scope of the Gupta dynasty (option 1). That the Guptas were ignorant or superstitious (option 2) is not implied and is contradicted by the passage's description of the Guptas' advancements in the arts and sciences. That Gupta scientists calculated the globe's circumference (option 4) and that Gupta poets produced famous verse (option 5) are not implications because they are directly stated in the passage.

6. **(5) Literature was intended for the enjoyment of all classes of society.** Option (5) is correct and can be implied from the statement in the passage indicating that literature was published in both common and elite languages, meaning literary materials were available to most Indians. The passage contradicts the ideas that many were illiterate during the Gupta dynasty (option 1), that poetry was not important (option 3), or that only scientists and religious leaders could read (option 4). The passage does not indicate that Indians were bilingual (option 2).

7. **(5) The Great Wall of China is a massive structure.** The huge size of the structure (option 5) is implied by the way the stone construction stretches far into the distant space shown in the photograph. There is no inference that special machines (option 1) were used to build the Great Wall. That the Chinese have always possessed superior technology (option 2) is not implied by the photograph. Option (3) is incorrect because the immense size of the wall and the battlements

along its top suggest that it was built for military defense—that the Chinese were indeed worried about invasion. The photograph does not imply what construction methods might have been relied upon by Chinese engineers (option 4).

KEY **Skill 4** Apply Ideas in a Different Context Pages 24–25

1. **(3) computer-related** Option (3) is correct because jobs related to computers had the highest percentage of growth. Option (1) is incorrect because jobs for personal care and home health aides, medical assistants, and physician assistants, while showing high percentage growth, did not grow as much as computer-related jobs. Option (2) is incorrect for the same reason: jobs in the legal field grew by a smaller percentage than those in computer-related fields. Option (4) is incorrect because the growth of manufacturing occupations is not indicated in the table. While jobs in human services (option 5) experienced growth, they did not grow as much as computer-related jobs did.

2. **(5) Department of Labor** Option (5) is correct because the Department of Labor is the government agency charged with preparing the American workforce for new and better jobs. The other options are incorrect because the Justice Department (option 1), Agriculture Department (option 2), Interior Department (option 3), and the State Department (option 4) are not responsible for preparing the American workforce for occupations.

3. **(5) the Fourteenth Amendment, which guarantees equal protection under the law for all citizens** The equal protection clause of the Fourteenth Amendment (option 5) was invoked because it is reasonable to conclude that if public schools were to provide equal education to all, then they should not include separate facilities for blacks and whites. The other options are incorrect because free speech (option 1), protection against unreasonable search and seizure (option 2), the right to a speedy trial (option 3), and the delegation of powers to states/people (option 4) do not address the idea of equality.

4. **(1) providing buses for black and white students to and from integrated public schools** Option (1) is correct because it would have resulted from the ruling requiring full equality in the field of public education. The other options are incorrect. Implementing standardized tests (option 2), lengthening the school day (option 3), eliminating arts and physical education classes (option 4), and tracking of high school students (option 5) would not address a mandate to provide equal access to all.

5. **(2) historical** Option (2) is correct because an instructor wishing to show the movement of the armies of Genghis Khan would need to use a map that shows events from the past. Option (1) is incorrect because political maps show borders between countries or states, not historical events. The other options are incorrect because physical maps (option 3) focus on landforms and water, relief maps (option 4) emphasize elevations, and road maps (option 5) show roads and distances.

6. **(5) road** Option (5) is correct because a person would need to consult a map of an area's roads in order to plan a truck's delivery route. The other options are incorrect because they

indicate political divisions (option 1), events from history (option 2), physical location of land and water (option 3), and elevation or geographic land features (option 4).

7. **(1) a committee on population relocation** Option (1) is correct; the title of the map reveals that it shows the proposed area for resettling Native Hawaiians, and the map highlights the proposed area in purple. Option (2) is incorrect. Because the area is still being "proposed," the resettlement hasn't happened yet; there is nothing on the map that would help a historian learn about Hawaii's history. Options (3), (4), and (5) are incorrect; the map does not show landforms, elevations, or roadways.

8. **(3) health standards for food production** Option (3) is a modern-day application of Progressive support for the improvement of citizens' rights. They would not support tax cuts for the wealthy (option 1) or limitations on workers' rights (option 2). Neither option (4) nor option (5) is related to improvements based on the Progressive outlook.

KEY **Skill 5** Make Inferences Pages 28–29

1. **(1) Imperialism was unfair because both parties did not benefit equally.** Option (1) is correct because the passage says colonizers exploited the resources of colonized countries and controlled native populations; this suggests the colonized gained less from imperialism than the colonizers. That colonizers felt compelled to educate their residents (option 2) is not suggested in the passage. The passage does not suggest that colonized countries benefited from the guidance of colonizers (option 3), but rather the opposite. The passage says that controlling native populations was "excused," implying imperialism did not always improve the lives of uncivilized people (option 4). The passage makes no suggestion that developing nations were eager to share natural resources (option 5).

2. **(5) disapproves of the concept** Option (5) is correct because the passage uses negative terms—for example, "air of superiority," "paternalism," "controlling native populations was excused"—to describe the concept of "the white man's burden," suggesting that the writer does not approve. That the writer agrees with (option 1), strongly favors (option 2), has mixed feelings about (option 3), or cares little about (option 4) the concept of "the white man's burden" are all contradicted by the negative terms used in the passage.

3. **(2) the uniformed white soldiers** Option (2) is correct because the uniformed white soldiers are shown fully dressed and seated on a platform above the partially clothed, bowing Africans, which strongly suggests their position of power. Option (1) is incorrect because the engraving does not show the tribal chiefs, so it is not possible to make inferences about their power. Option (3) is incorrect because the soldiers' positions and body language suggest they are the more powerful. Option (4) is incorrect because the spectators include both uniformed white soldiers and Africans, and nothing in the engraving suggests the group of spectators is the most powerful. Option (5) is incorrect because only one group can be the most powerful.

4. **(4) with disdain** Option (4) is correct because the white soldiers' unfriendly posture and expressions seem to

suggest that they "look down upon," or lack respect for, and openly dislike the Africans. Option (1) is contradicted by the engraving, which seems to suggest the soldiers lack respect for the Africans. Nothing in the etching suggests that the soldiers hate the Africans (option 2). While the soldiers may view the Africans with tolerance (option 3), this idea is not suggested by anything in the engraving. Option (5) is incorrect because the white soldiers do not appear to admire the Africans.

5. **(4) They were forced to give up their best lands to non–Native Americans.** Option (4) is correct; by stating that the U.S. government placed the Native Americans on reservations in remote, less desirable areas, the passage suggests that Native Americans were forced to give up their best lands. Option (1) is incorrect because the passage does not make suggestions about Native Americans' feelings. Option (2) is incorrect because moving Native Americans to less desirable areas does not suggest that the U.S. government made an effort to treat them fairly. Option (3) is incorrect because the passage does not suggest that other ethnic groups were placed on reservations. Option (5) is incorrect because the passage states that conflicts were ongoing—not avoided.

6. **(2) Native Americans have been victims of the U.S. government's decision to place them on reservations.** Option (2) is correct. By stating that Native Americans lived in America and governed themselves before being placed on reservations, the passage suggests that Native Americans were victims in a deal that hurt them and helped the U.S. government. Option (1) is not correct; nothing in the passage suggests Native Americans benefited from interactions with the U.S. government. Option (3) is incorrect because the passage says the areas were not desirable. While the passage says Native Americans signed agreements with the colonists, nothing suggests that Native Americans welcomed the colonists' form of government (option 4). While it is true that Native American cultures are varied, option (5) is incorrect because it is not suggested by the passage.

7. **(3) Some individuals profit at the expense of other people's work.** Option (3) is correct because the facts of the cartoon—a poor and weary labor force trudging behind a cigar-smoking, money-clutching rich man—suggest that the people who do the hard work aren't necessarily the people who profit from that work. The cartoon does not imply that working people are pleased with their jobs (option 1) but rather the opposite, as indicated by the workers' negative facial expressions. The inference that people will follow a strong leader (option 2) is incorrect because the man at the head of the line is depicted as greedy, not strong. Options (4) and (5) are incorrect because nothing in the cartoon suggests the idea of a union or the construction industry.

KEY **Skill 6 Identify Facts and Opinions Pages 32–33**

1. **(1) It led to the deaths of thousands of Americans and Vietnamese.** Option (1) is correct because it can be confirmed in the historical record. While it is true that the Vietnamese New Year is called Tet, option (2) does not relate

to the broken cease-fire. Option (3) is untrue and contradicts information in the passage about Americans' reactions. Option (4) misinterprets the assertion, cited by McCarthy, that in 1965 the enemy had been defeated. While McCarthy said "the fact is the enemy is bolder than ever" (option 5), this is actually an opinion about the enemy's feelings, not a fact.

2. **(2) The U.S. government continued to make hollow claims of progress and victory.** Option (2) is correct because it is an opinion expressed by McCarthy. The judgment word *hollow* is a signal that this is an opinion. When the Vietnamese New Year is (option 1), that Tet shocked U.S. citizens (option 3), that the North Vietnamese broke the cease-fire (option 4), and that both Americans and Vietnamese were killed (option 5) are all facts that can be confirmed.

3. **(2) The prison population more than doubled from 1980 to 1990.** Option (2) is correct because the graph indicates the number of inmates went from less than 500 thousand in 1980 to more than one million in 1990. That the courts are doing a good job (option 1), not enough prisons are being built (option 3), and more prisoners should be paroled (option 5) are opinions not measured on the graph. Option (4) is incorrect because the graph does not measure crime rate.

4. **(3) More guards are needed.** Option (3) is correct because it is the opinion of many people from the last sentence of the passage. Options (1) and (4) are not addressed as opinions in the passage. Option (2) is incorrect because it contradicts the opinion that adding guards will help the situation. Option (5) is not an opinion of the passage but a fact that can be confirmed.

5. **(3) Competition works better than any other economic system.** Option (3) is correct. It is an opinion based on the statement in the passage that competition serves the needs of both individuals and society. The judgment word *better* signals that this is an opinion. Option (1) is incorrect because the passage does not state specific opinions about the U.S. economic system. The role of competition in keeping prices down (option 2) and competition's effect on wages (option 4) are not opinions but facts of economic theory. Option (5) is not an opinion but a misstated fact—under competition the maximum number of goods will be produced at the best prices.

6. **(1) Automobile manufacturers compete with each other for the consumer's business.** Option (1) is correct because, as described by the passage, competition refers to any interaction between buyers and sellers. Option (2) is contradicted by the idea that rivalry in the marketplace keeps things in balance. While the passage states that a job seeker who asks for more than the usual wage will not get the job, the passage does not mention asking for a raise (option 3) in a competitive market. Option (4) is incorrect because the passage states that a job seeker who asks more than the usual wage will not get the job. It does not state that the job will go to the worker who accepts the lowest wage. Option (5) is contradicted by the passage.

7. **(5) White males have nothing to complain about when it comes to their role in the construction business.** Option (5) is correct because it is an opinion based on the information provided. That firms owned by

white males earned the most (option 1); white female-owned firms earned the least (option 2), minority- and white female owned firms combined earned about 10% of the total paid for construction services (option 3) and were paid a combined total of $20 million (option 4) are facts indicated by the graphs.

Skill 7 Recognize Unstated Assumptions Pages 36–37

1. **(3) Not all employers provide insurance to their workers.** Option (3) is correct as suggested by the total percentage of workers—only 57.1—who have employment-based health insurance. Options (1), (2), (4), and (5) are not addressed by the graph.

2. **(2) They are less likely to offer insurance.** Option (2) is correct as suggested by the graph, which shows that companies with fewer than 25 employees offer health benefits to fewer of their employees than larger companies. Options (1), (3), (4), and (5) are not indicated by the graph.

3. **(3) Fish are a major source of food for many of the world's people.** Option (3) is correct; according to the passage, coastal areas are heavily populated because of the availability of fish, a resource. In order to understand why this resource is important, a reader must know that many people eat fish. Option (1) is incorrect because there is no information about how coastal dwellers earn their living. Option (2) is only true for some coastal regions and does not relate to the passage. Option (4) confuses facts from the passage—polar regions have no trees; there is no mention of trees in coastal areas. Option (5) may be true but is not an assumption based on the information in the passage.

4. **(2) a denial of credit** Option (2) is correct because if a person is denied credit, it is likely due to negative information contained in a credit report. Options (1), (3), (4), and (5) are incorrect because they are not relevant to the passage.

5. **(1) A good, accurate credit rating carries great importance.** Option (1) is correct because negative or incorrect information in an individual's credit file increases the chances that he or she will be denied credit. Options (2), (3), and (4) are incorrect because they are not supported by the passage. While it is true that consumers are entitled to privacy in their business dealings (option 5), this is not the basic assumption underlying the Fair Credit Reporting Act.

6. **(3) It is designed to protect consumers.** Option (3) is correct because the U.S. Fair Credit Reporting Act allows individuals to inspect and challenge items in their credit files. Options (1) and (2) are incorrect because they contradict the passage. Options (4) and (5) are incorrect and not relevant to the passage.

7. **(2) impoverished and oppressed** Option (2) is correct because it is reasonable to assume that a life of such discrimination and restriction would lead to impoverishment and oppression. Option (1) is incorrect and contradicts the text, which indicates black citizens in South Africa during apartheid were discriminated against and faced heavy restrictions in their everyday activities. Option (3) is incorrect. The idea of longevity is not relevant to the passage, and the passage contradicts the statement that life during apartheid was rewarding for black citizens. Option (4) is incorrect because the assumption contradicts the information in the

passage and the table. Option (5) is incorrect because it is not relevant to the passage.

Skill 8 Identify Causes and Effects Pages 40–41

1. **(4) the burning of fossil fuels and destruction of forests** Option (4) is correct because it correctly identifies from the first paragraph the factors that raise CO_2 levels, the gas that regulates the atmosphere. Options (1) and (2) describe effects of global warming, not causes. Option (3) is incorrect based on the passage; global warming is the result of increased CO_2 gas levels. Option (5) mixes a cause and effect together.

2. **(1) Global warming could decrease the land area where people live.** Option (1) is correct because it accurately restates a cause-and-effect relationship presented in the second paragraph. Options (2), (3), and (4) are incorrect because they reverse the cause-and-effect relationship. Option (5) is not addressed in the passage.

3. **(3) Commercial air travel became a popular form of transportation.** Option (3) is correct, as suggested by the last sentence of the passage. While options (1) and (2) may be true, neither is the lasting result of Lindbergh's flight nor mentioned in the passage. Options (4) and (5) are not supported by the photograph or passage.

4. **(2) The public became fascinated with airplanes.** Option (2) is correct as indicated by the crowd shown in the photograph—they were there to see the flight of the *Spirit of St. Louis.* The large crowd is not an indication of whether people like to gather in large crowds (option 1). Options (3) and (5) are not supported by the photograph. Option (4) contradicts the photograph.

5. **(4) It slows down the economy.** Option (4) is correct. Because supply-side economists believe that lower taxes lead to economic growth, they would also believe that higher taxes slow the economy. Options (1), (3), and (5) are not addressed in or supported by the passage. Option (2) is the opposite of the correct answer.

6. **(1) a reduction in funds for food stamps and Medicaid** Option (1) is correct because one concern of supply-side critics is that tax cuts penalize the poor and decrease the amount of money the government has to spend. Food stamps and Medicaid are government-funded programs designed to ensure that low-income families eat properly and get medical care. Options (2), (3), (4), and (5) are not supported by information in the passage.

7. **(3) Most of Earth's surface is water while less than one-third of the surface is land.** Option (3) is correct because as the chart indicates, 70% of Earth's surface is covered by oceans. Options (1) and (4) are not addressed by the chart. Option (2) is contradicted by the chart, which indicates tillable land makes up only 6% of Earth's surface. Option (5) is contradicted by the chart's indication that oceans make up 70% of Earth's surface.

8. **(1) increased demand on the tillable land** Option (1) is correct because an increased population would increase demand for food, which is grown on tillable land. Options (2), (3), (4), and (5) are not addressed in the data included in the chart.

Skill 9 Draw Conclusions
Pages 44–45

1. **(3) Economic issues influenced Southerners' attitudes toward slavery.** Option (3) is correct because the passage states that Southerners began to defend slavery when they realized their improved economy relied on slave labor. That the cotton gin promoted the end of slavery (option 1) and that Americans were never in favor of slavery (option 2) are contradicted in the passage. The Southerners' morality (option 4) and the actual treatment of slaves (option 5) are not mentioned.

2. **(5) The Northern economy relied less on slave labor than the Southern economy did.** Option (5) is correct. As indicated by the table, cotton was not a major crop of the North; thus, the Northern economy did not rely on slave labor. Northerners' humanity (option 1), whether or not they were British citizens (option 2), and the proportion of abolitionists living in the North (option 4) are all unrelated to the information in the table. Option (3) is contradicted by information in the table.

3. **(2) Food preferences are often determined by cultural influences.** Option (2) is correct because the passage states that our attitudes about things are based on the culture in which we live. Options (1) and (3) contradict the passage, which says that eating beef is unthinkable to Hindus. Option (4) is incorrect because the passage does not suggest that Hindus would ever eat beef. Option (5) is incorrect and contradicts the passage, which says that North Americans enjoy eating beef.

4. **(3) Southern cities were utterly devastated by the war.** Option (3) is supported by the destroyed city block shown in the photograph and the "total war" destruction of Southern public works described in the passage. Option (1) is incorrect because neither the photograph nor the passage gives information to suggest the South did not plan to defend its cities. Option (2) is directly contradicted by the passage, which describes a "collapse" of the Confederate army and "complete victory" for the Union. Option (4) is also contradicted by the passage, which describes "total war" as a strategy implemented by Union, not Confederate, forces. Option (5) is contradicted by the passage, which says the Union attacked civilian areas such as fields, factories, homes, and railroads.

5. **(2) believed "total war" was necessary for victory** Option (2) is correct because the passage indicates Sherman made a decision to practice "total war." Option (1) is incorrect because Sherman attacked non-military targets such as fields, factories, homes, and railroads. While Sherman may have called Southerners a "hostile people," it is not suggested by the photograph or passage that he hated all of them (option 3). The photograph and passage do not indicate that Sherman cared about war's effects on civilians (option 4) or that he followed accepted rules of warfare (option 5).

6. **(5) a wealthy suburb** Option (5) is correct. The passage states that there is a link between income level and voting, and a suburb where the wealthy live is likely to have a bigger turnout of eligible voters. Option (1) is incorrect because it is directly contradicted by the passage, which states that the lower-income population is less likely to vote. The passage provides no information about the voting behavior of college students (option 2), retirees (option 3), or women (option 4).

7. **(1) an income tax break** Option (1) is correct because even in a district with people from all incomes, high-income voters would be more likely to vote than others; they would stand to gain the most financially from an income tax break. Option (2) is incorrect because no one is likely to benefit from paying increased property taxes. Options (3) and (4) are incorrect because those whose families are most likely to benefit from school lunch programs or expanded welfare benefits are also those who are less likely to vote. Option (5) is incorrect because the higher income people are most likely to vote, and they would not gain financially if low-income households paid less taxes.

Skill 10 Evaluate Support for Generalizations Pages 48–49

1. **(4) Deciphering Mayan glyphs was difficult with so few resources available.** Option (4) is correct; that most Mayan books were destroyed supports the conclusion that the glyphs were hard to interpret until recently. There is no evidence in the passage that the bishop spared the four "best" books (option 1). Option (2) is not relevant to the fact that most Mayan books were destroyed. That scholars did not try to understand the glyphs until recently (option 3) is not supported by the passage. While it is true that the glyphs are complicated (option 5), the passage does not indicate a connection between the glyphs' complexity and their destruction.

2. **(5) The Mayans developed a complex mathematical system.** Option (5) is correct because the Mayans' development of a complex mathematical system indicates a high degree of advancement. Option (1) is incorrect because the geographic distribution does not necessarily relate to degree of intellectual advancement. Option (2) is incorrect; even though the Mayans defeated the Spaniards, it does not relate to the advancement of Mayan society. Option (3) does not relate to the Mayans' degree of intellectual advancement. Option (4) supports their development of a belief system rather than their intellectual advancement.

3. **(1) Early Egyptians were a skilled, industrious people.** Option (1) is correct because the painting shows figures clearly involved in a work activity resulting in the creation of jewelry. Option (2) is incorrect; there is no evidence to suggest that all Egyptians owned jewelry. Option (3) is incorrect; while the information notes the painting was from the tomb of Sebekhotep, there is nothing to indicate that he painted it. The other options are incorrect, as nothing in the painting supports the conclusions that the Egyptians had quantities of gold (option 4) or that all Egyptian tombs contained artwork (option 5).

4. **(3) New technology and economic issues affect each other in complex ways.** Option (3) is correct because as the passage states, new medical technology raises economic issues at the same time insurers are limiting the coverage they will provide for such care. Option (1) is incorrect because the passage indicates the opposite—that the development of such systems does face economic

restraints. Option (2) is incorrect because the passage does not indicate that economic issues have more impact than ethical issues. Options (4) and (5) are incorrect, as the passage does not address how many people seek life support despite ethical dilemmas or whether people are entitled to artificial life support.

5. **(2) Hammurabi advocated harsh penalties for crimes.** Option (2) is correct because as the passage states, Hammurabi's legal code was based on a concept of severe punishment. Option (1) is incorrect; while Hammurabi may have been "ruthless," the passage more directly supports the idea of his tough approach to crime and punishment. Option (3) is incorrect because nothing in the passage suggests that the stone slab was not an authentic artifact. The other options are incorrect, as there are no statements in the passage to suggest that the Babylonians were especially violent (option 4) or that many of Hammurabi's laws are still used today (option 5).

6. **(4) Destruction of rain forests has occurred at a surprisingly rapid pace.** Option (4) is correct; as the cartoon indicates, in a mere 10 years the rain forest has been completely replaced by a city. The other options are incorrect, as nothing in the cartoon indicates that traffic problems have increased (option 1), what people's living preferences might be (option 2), the relative importance of cities and rain forests (option 3), or that people have been suffering (option 5).

7. **(5) It has damaged Earth's natural habitats.** Option (5) is correct because the cartoon shows a crowded cityscape of buildings, bridges, and roads covering the previously natural land. The other options are incorrect; the cartoon gives no clues about the standard of living of native peoples before and after urbanization (option 1), the degree to which the natural environment has been preserved (option 2), the city providing much-needed jobs (option 3), or Earth's beauty before and after this urban development (option 4).

Skill 11 Tables and Charts
Pages 52–53

1. **(4) Funding favors areas that produce revenue rather than those that provide a public service.** Option (4) is the best restatement of the information in the table. While the increased spending for school construction seems to support the idea that the state financially supports and values education (option 1), this is not the best answer given that while raising money for school construction, the state is making huge cuts in public school funding. Option (2) is incorrect because whether the state previously over-funded the education system cannot be determined from the table, which shows a snapshot of a single budget without any historical reference. Nothing in the table suggests that funding favors the elderly (option 3). That the state's roads are in heavy need of repair (option 5) is not indicated by the table; the huge budget addition for highway construction probably refers to new highway construction rather than repair.

2. **(4) Schools will not be able to operate.** The reduction of more than $250 million from public school funding will likely make it difficult for schools to pay their bills and continue operation. Option (1) is contradicted by the chart, which shows $223 million for school construction. Option (2) is incorrect; it is not likely that a $250 million budget cut would not affect how schools operate. Option (3) is incorrect because the table does not address future cuts in education or other budgets. While it is possible that classes get larger or programs get cut (option 5), this is not the best option; the bigger problem would be that schools throughout the state may be unable to continue operating at all.

3. **(5) The number of business investments and the jobs that follow will increase.** Option (5) correctly identifies a likely intended effect of the tax incentives, which could make investing by businesses less costly and thus more profitable while also generating new jobs. Options (1) and (2) are incorrect because nothing in the table points to the idea of increased taxes or economic stimulus checks. Option (3) is incorrect because the table does not address the subject of private investment for schools. Option (4) is not the best answer because while new business construction is a desired effect of the tax incentives, this is only part of a larger intended effect—business investments and the jobs that come with it.

4. **(1) The state is attempting to jump-start its economy.** Option (1) follows logically from the information in the table. The budget additions for tax incentives seem to indicate the state is investing heavily in promoting business investment, the general conditions for which probably involve an underperforming economy. Nothing in the table indicates whether the state is attempting to balance its budget (option 2), whether the state has a progressive educational system (option 3), or that the state is levying additional taxes (option 4). Option (5) is incorrect because it is clear from the table that the state is funding at least some programs, such as substance abuse and work training, and thus it is not cutting funding to all programs.

5. **(1) cut back on programs** Option (1) is correct; without federal money such as grants and revenue sharing, states would not have as much money to fund their programs. With less money, states would not be financially independent (option 2) or have better public transportation (option 5). Option (3) is incorrect because block grants are a form of federal money that would be lacking if federal money became unavailable. Option (4) is incorrect because local libraries would be under local control.

6. **(2) taxes** Option (2) is correct; as shown by the chart, state and local funds are raised through taxes. Options (1), (3), (4) and (5) are incorrect because they are all federal, not local, sources of funding.

7. **(5) special revenue sharing** Option (5) is correct. The question states that the mayor received federal money, and the chart shows that special revenue sharing is a type of federal money for purposes such as transportation without a requirement that local government contribute matching money of its own. The funding could not have come from a categorical grant-in-aid (option 1) because that grant requires a matching contribution, and the question says the city did not have to pay. Options (2) and (4) are incorrect because block grants and general revenue sharing are types of federal money granted to state, not local, governments. Option (3) is incorrect. Per the chart, taxes are state and local money, and the question says the mayor received federal money.

8. **(1) a categorical grant-in-aid** Option (1) is correct because the question says the state had to match part of the money, and the chart shows this match is required with categorical grants-in-aid. Options (2) and (5) are incorrect because block grants and general revenue sharing do not require a state match in funds. Option (3) is incorrect. Taxes are raised at state and local level, but the question says the state received money from a federal program. Option (4) is incorrect because special revenue sharing is federal money given to local, not state, governments.

KEY Skill 12 Bar Graphs
Pages 56–57

1. **(2) The distance between Japan and the United States does not prevent millions of Japanese from traveling here.** Option (2) correctly applies information from the graph showing millions of Japanese visited the United States in 2006. The graph provides no information about the preferences of travelers (options 1 and 3), the reasons why people travel to United States (option 4), or visits to other countries (option 5).

2. **(1) the total population between 18 and 65 years old** Option (1) is correct because the graph shows only the population younger than age 18 and older than age 65. The graph already shows the population between age 5 and age 18 (option 2). Information about people who moved to or from California in 2006 or the total number of births in the state in that year (options 3, 4, and 5) would not help determine the total estimated population of the state.

3. **(4) Young people deserve attention in California.** Option (4) is correct. The graph shows that the population under age 18 is roughly 12 million, so the graph could be used to support the statement that the needs of young people deserve attention. The graph gives no information about the state's birth rate (option 1) or about how much of the population 65 and over is retired (option 2). Options (3) and (5) are incorrect because the graph does not give enough information to predict future population trends in California.

4. **(4) nearly a C** Option (4) is correct. The bar representing all adults' opinion of public schools in the nation at large nearly reaches the line labeled 2, indicating the grade C. Options (1), (2), and (3) are incorrect because they state grades higher than the graph shows. Option (5) is incorrect because it states a grade lower than the graph shows.

5. **(3) Adults generally have a higher opinion of local schools than of schools in the nation at large.** Option (3) is correct. For every group of adults, the bar representing the grade for local schools is higher than the bar representing the grade for schools in the nation at large. Option (1) is incorrect, and contradicted by the graph. The graph doesn't address information about private schools (options 2 and 5), or how many adults have children in school or how many do not (option 4).

6. **(3) A negligible source of energy in 1950, nuclear power was the source of more energy than renewable sources in 2000.** Option (3) is correct because the graph shows no energy use from nuclear power in 1950, and the bar representing energy use from nuclear power in 2000 is higher than the bar showing energy use from

renewable sources in 2000. The energy use from renewable sources in 2000, added to the energy use from fossil fuels in 2000, is less than four times the energy use from fossil fuels in 1950 (option 1). The graph gives no information about the impact of conservation efforts (option 2). Options (4) and (5) are incorrect because the consumption of energy from renewable sources and from fossil fuels less than tripled from 1950 to 2000.

7. **(2) Energy consumption from all sources more than doubled from 1950 to 2000.** Option (2) correctly states information supported by the graph: each of the bars for consumption in 2000 is at least twice as high as the bar for 1950. That the attempt to decrease the use of fossil fuels in favor of renewable sources has failed (option 1) is an opinion, not a fact supported by the graph. The graph gives no information about the reliability of the sources of energy (option 3). The graph does not provide enough information to make a prediction about long-term trends in the use of nuclear power (option 4) or about the future use of fossil fuels (option 5).

KEY Skill 13 Line Graphs
Pages 60–61

1. **(5) The percent of households with computers has increased each year since 1997.** Option (5) accurately restates the information displayed on the graph, which shows the percentage of households with computers steadily rising from 1997 to 2003. Option (1) is not correct because the percentage of households with computers in 2003 is less than double that of 1997. Option (2) is incorrect because the increase from 1997 to 1998 was greater. Option (3) cannot be assumed from the graph because the graph doesn't say which households purchased computers for the first time in 1999. Option (4) is not correct because the graph gives no information about the cost of computers.

2. **(3) increased steadily** Only option (3) correctly states a continuation of the trend shown in the graph, which is that the percent of households with computers steadily increased from 1997 to 2003. Options (1), (2), (4), and (5) state changes from this trend.

3. **(4) 2004** Option (4) is correct because from 2004 to 2005 the center saw sharp increases in the enrollment of students whose native languages are Spanish or Japanese. Option (1) is incorrect because from 2001 to 2002 the enrollment of students whose native languages are Spanish or Japanese remained steady. Options (2) and (3) are incorrect because from 2002 to 2004 the enrollment of students whose native language is Spanish increased slightly while the enrollment of students whose native language is Japanese remained steady. Option (5) is incorrect because from 2005 to 2006 the enrollment of students whose native language is Japanese increased while the enrollment of students whose native language is Spanish remained steady.

4. **(2) The center must address the needs of students whose native language is not English.** Option (2) is correct. It is clear from the graph that the center has increasing numbers of native Spanish and Japanese speakers; to be effective the center must address the needs of the students it has. Option (1) is incorrect because the center still serves

roughly 250 native English speakers. Options (3), (4), and (5) are incorrect because the graph gives no information about unemployment rates, enrollment at the local community college, or class offerings at the center.

5. **(2) 300 tons** Option (2) is correct because the rate of increase from 2000 to 2005 is about 50 tons. The amount of material recycled in 2005 was 250 tons; add 50 tons to predict a total of 300 tons in 2010. Option (1) has the amount of material recycled in 2010 the same as the amount in 2005; this would be true only if there were a change from the trend shown in the graph. Options (3), (4), and (5) also represent changes from the trend shown in the graph, with the amount of recycling increasing at a much greater rate than in previous years.

6. **(5) the population of the county in 2005 as compared to the population in 1980** Only option (5) correctly states information that would help county leaders. The increasing rate of recycling could be due to population growth; to determine whether the trend shown in the graph means that the individuals in the county are recycling more, leaders would need to compare the change in population with the change in the amount of recycling. Options (1), (2), (3), and (4) are incorrect because the information suggested in the options would not reveal anything about the numbers of individuals recycling in Jefferson County or about the amount that individuals recycle.

7. **(3) Kershaw County was able to reduce its utility rates.** Option (3) is correct because there was a reduction in utility bills in Kershaw County from 2005 to 2006 and 2007. Options (1) and (2) are incorrect because the graph does not provide complete information about the cost of living in either county. Options (4) and (5) are incorrect because they are based on information that the graph does not provide, such as whether every home in Charleston County received electricity or complaints in Kershaw County.

KEY Skill 14 Circle Graphs
Pages 64–65

1. **(4) Though they make up half of the management force in today's business world, women are underrepresented in the executive jobs at top companies.** Option (4) correctly uses information from both graphs to reach a logical conclusion. While it may be true that women have come a long way to be able to serve as chief executives (option 1), this is an opinion, not a conclusion based on information in the graphs. Likewise, the statements that women do not make good chief executives (option 2) or that women would make the best chief executives if only given the chance (option 5) are opinions and thus incorrect. The statement that the reason more women are not hired as chief executives is because of gender prejudice in top companies (option 3) identifies a possible cause-and-effect relationship that is not supported by information in the graphs.

2. **(1) The number of micro business loans fell from 21.6 million in 2006 to 19 million in 2007.** Option (1) correctly restates information from the graphs about the number of small business loans in 2006 and 2007. Options (2) and (4) may be true but are not the correct answers because that information cannot be found in the graphs. Options (3) and (5) are incorrect and contradicted by information in the graphs.

3. **(1) No candidate won at least 50% of the popular vote.** Option (1) is most relevant to the final decision of the election because Andrew Jackson did not have enough electoral votes to win without a majority of the popular vote. While it is true that 261 electoral votes were cast in the 1824 election (option 2), this is not the best option because it doesn't include the factor of the percentage of majority vote received. The statement that all of the candidates were part of the same political party (option 3) is incorrect and irrelevant to the outcome of the election. The fact that both popular and electoral votes have always been used in election results (option 4) is not the most relevant option. While it is true that four candidates were contenders in the 1824 presidential election (option 5), this fact is not the most relevant to the outcome of the election.

4. **(4) 37** Option (4) is correct. The passage states that Clay gave his electoral votes to Adams, and the graph indicates Clay had 37 votes. Option (1) is incorrect because 47,136 represents the popular vote total for Clay, not the electoral vote. Options (2), (3), and (5) are incorrect because 46,618, 41, and 14 are the popular and electoral vote totals for Crawford and the electoral vote percentage for Clay, not the actual number of electoral votes for Clay.

5. **(2) 261** Option (2) is correct; as indicated by the electoral vote graph, candidates Jackson, Adams, Crawford, and Clay had 99, 84, 41, and 37 votes, respectively, for a total of 261. Option (1) refers inaccurately to the popular vote total, which was 356,038, not 356,040. Options (3), (4), and (5) are incorrect because they don't add up the electoral vote total but seem to refer to other numbers from the graphs, such as the number of electoral votes received by Jackson and Adams.

6. **(3) The Electoral College makes the final decision on presidential elections.** Option (3) correctly states that the Electoral College, who cast the electoral votes, have the final decision on presidential elections; this can be seen in the fact that Jackson won the popular vote but did not garner enough electoral votes to secure the presidency. Options (1), (2), and (4) are incorrect and directly contradicted in the passage: Jackson did win the highest popular vote and was not elected president; Adams ended up getting more electoral votes than his popular vote earned him; and clearly a plurality of votes, which Jackson had, is not as good as a majority. Option (5) is untrue and not a conclusion that can be drawn from the passage and graphs.

Skill 15 Photographs
Pages 68–69

1. **(3) isolationism** Option (3) is correct because the photograph shows Roosevelt signing a declaration of war against Japan, which signals a change from the U.S. being isolated, or neutral, in the war. The other options are incorrect because nothing in the photograph or caption refer in any way to the Truman Doctrine (option 1), immigration laws (option 2), military benefits (option 4), or financial support for education (option 5).

2. **(1) increased military costs** Option (1) best describes a change directly related to going to war against Japan: the increased military costs that the war would require. Option (2) is opposite the correct answer. The other answers are

incorrect because there is no logical connection between increased housing costs (option 3), increased education costs (option 4), or decreased education costs (option 5) and the declaration of war on Japan.

3. **(2) A major social issue in today's workforce is balancing a career with family.** Option (2) is correct. The caption "The New Workforce" beneath the photograph of a woman holding a baby and a briefcase, as if she is leaving home for work, indicate that making room in life for both family and a professional career is a social issue of today. Option (1) is incorrect because the photograph and caption do not suggest that all women must work in order to have enough money to live comfortably. Option (3) is incorrect because nothing in the photograph or caption suggests that women are happier working than raising families. Option (4) is incorrect and contradicted by the caption and photograph. The caption describes the subject of the photograph as a "new" workforce—meaning a different or changed force of workers. Option (5) is incorrect because the photograph shows a woman whose clothing and briefcase indicate she is not a factory worker but a professional.

4. **(1) providing onsite daycare** Option (1) would show that a company values its workers and wants to make life more convenient for workers with young children. Option (2) is incorrect. While paying workers more might show commitment to them, restricting the family leave time would make life harder for a working mother and would not be likely to encourage employees to stay. Requiring more overtime (option 3) would not help a company keep employees. While improving the insurance coverage offered to workers (option 4) is helpful, increasing workers' insurance costs accordingly does not show commitment to the workers or improve their life but rather adds a financial burden. Option (5) is incorrect because providing mentors for only male employees would make many other employees angry.

5. **(1) higher hourly pay** Option (1) is correct. The woman's sign suggests one reason she is on strike is because her employer, Mid City Realty, underpays its workers. This leads to the conclusion that she would find higher pay desirable. While workers might go on strike in search of fewer hours (option 2), an end to discrimination (option 3), better working conditions (option 4), or more health insurance (option 5), none of these choices is the best answer because none reflect the emphasis on underpayment on the sign.

6. **(3) picketing** Option (3) is correct; the woman's sign in support of the strike against Mid City Realty indicates she is a picketer—someone who posts a picket, or sign, to argue for a change. Options (1), (2), and (5) are incorrect. Nothing in the photograph shows that the people are in violent confrontation, lobbying for a political change, or not using a product. While the picketers may have met in one place, option (4) is not the best answer, as the three figures in the photograph do not appear to be at a meeting.

7. **(1) oppression versus freedom** Option (1) is correct. The wall separating communist East Berlin from democratic West Berlin was a physical symbol of the division between communism, or oppression, and freedom. The other options are incorrect because nothing in the photograph or question suggests that the wall was a symbol of diversity (option 2), the

end of World War II (option 3), free trade (option 4), or open-door relations among nations (option 5).

8. **(3) could not move freely to and from each other's part of the city** Option (3) is correct; the wall physically stopped people from passing from East to West Berlin. Option (1) is incorrect and opposite the correct answer. While the females in the photograph wear scarves and the man a suit (option 2), nothing in the photograph indicates that all East and West Berliners were required to wear these clothes. While citizens of both East and West Berlin were known to try to climb over the Berlin Wall (option 4) and were often shot at by those who guarded it (option 5), this is not shown in the photograph.

KEY Skill 16 Timelines and Drawings
Pages 72–73

1. **(3) Buffalo were killed as white civilization moved westward.** Option (3) is correct as implied by the drawing, titled "The Far West," which shows the shooting of buffalo as a steam engine train makes its way across the countryside. The other options are incorrect because the drawing does not indicate that Indians hunted buffalo (option 1), the buffalo were killed for food (option 2), they are extinct today (option 4), or that they originated from the area now known as Montana (option 5).

2. **(5) Cars cost more to drive than mopeds.** Option (5) is the best conclusion because the drawing shows a car with many dollar signs above it and a moped with only one dollar sign above it, leading to the conclusion that a car is more expensive than a moped. Options (1) and (3) are incorrect because nothing in the drawing refers to your vehicle influencing income or credit. Option (2) is incorrect because it is the opposite of the correct conclusion. Option (4) is incorrect because while a car may be more expensive than a moped, the drawing does not suggest that it is too expensive for ordinary people to afford.

3. **(4) As an ally of Serbia, Russia mobilized its armies.** Option (4) is correct because the timeline shows that Russia entered the war in 1914, just after Austria-Hungary declared war on Serbia in July 1914. Options (1) and (2) are incorrect and contradicted by information in the timeline, which shows that the U.S. entry into the war and the overthrow of the Czarist government by the Bolsheviks both occurred in 1917, well after war was declared in 1914. Option (3) is incorrect because, per the timeline, Archduke Ferdinand was assassinated before Austria-Hungary declared war on Serbia. Option (5) is incorrect because Option (4) is correct.

4. **(2) The First World War was a time of great turmoil.** Option (2) is correct and based on the information in the timeline that shows World War I included both violent battles and revolution. That women did not participate in the war (option 1) is contradicted by the timeline, which notes that women joined the WAAC in Britain in 1917. While Verdun and the Somme (option 3) were long and deadly battles, the timeline doesn't suggest that these were the bloodiest battles in history. Options (4) and (5) are incorrect and contradicted by the timeline, which suggests that Germany was at war with England and France and therefore not an ally of either country.

5. (2) The U.S. entered the war later than the other countries. Option (2) is correct because it restates information from the timeline that shows the U.S. did not declare war until 1917, whereas Russia, Germany, France, and Britain went to war in 1914. That the U.S. was not involved in the war (option 1) or entered the war before other countries (option 3) is incorrect and contradicted by the timeline. That the U.S. entered the war because Wilson was criticized for not joining the fight (option 4) is incorrect and can't be known from the timeline. While it is true that Wilson was a Democrat, option (5) is incorrect because it can't be inferred from the timeline.

6. (2) Wars include both men and women. Option (2) is correct because, as the timeline shows, British women had joined the war effort by 1917. The timeline contradicts the statement that wars included men only (option 1). The statements that women did not take part in wars until World War II (option 3) or Vietnam (option 4) are contradicted by the timeline as noted. The timeline does not suggest anything about only women fighting wars of the future (option 5).

KEY **Skill 17 Political Cartoons**
Pages 76–77

1. (5) The meaning of the donkey and the elephant as political symbols depends upon the opinion of the audience. Option (5) is correct because as the cartoon shows, the elephant and the donkey see each other opposite how they see themselves. Options (1), (2), and (3) are incorrect because as the cartoon indicates, the donkey and elephant are not fixed symbols for the positive or the negative. Similarly, not all voters always view the donkey as always clever and courageous (option 4).

2. (1) Korea is both stuck in the past and trying to move toward the future. Option (1) is correct because as the cartoon suggests, today's Korea, divided by poor North and wealthy South, is stuck in the past while it tries to move forward into the future. The statement that Korea is a giant ready to take on the world (option 2) is not supported by the cartoon. The statement that North Korea's nuclear capacity is a grave concern of its enemies (option 3) is true but is not information from the cartoon. Options (4) and (5) are incorrect and contradict the cartoon.

3. (2) Young people deserve to be addressed and engaged by the political process. Option (2) correctly identifies the main inference of the cartoon. There is nothing in the cartoon to indicate the cartoonist feels young people are being picky (option 1). Nothing in the cartoon implies that young people ages 18 to 21 have never been a major voting bloc (option 3). While the young people in the cartoon are showing emotion, the cartoon does not imply they are too emotional (option 4). The statement that young voters are more likely to be democrats (option 5) is not implied by the cartoon.

4. (1) If young voters are given inspiring choices in 2012, they will be back to vote in 2016. Option (1) best supports the information in the cartoon, including the title and the captions that indicate if young people have engaging choices, they will be likely to continue to vote in the future. That voters would not vote in the future (option 2) is opposite the correct answer. While candidates can affect voter turnout

(option 3), this is not the best assumption; there are not more voters in the frame with more candidates. That Democrats are always the same as Republicans (option 4) is not implied by the cartoon. The statement that young people are not political anymore (option 5) is incorrect and not implied by the cartoon.

5. (2) When young people are engaged in elections, they turn out to vote, and they will make a habit of voting in the future. Option (2) logically follows from the information presented in the cartoons. The conclusion that young people may turn out to vote but then never vote again (option 1) is not logical based on the cartoon. While it's true young voters may have the power to impact a vote (option 3), this is not the best conclusion because it is not addressed in the cartoon. The statement that young people will still turn out to vote, even if not faced with interesting choices (option 4), is contradicted by the cartoon. The statement that democrats and republicans don't hold the interest of young people (option 5) is not a logical conclusion of the cartoon.

KEY **Skill 18 Maps**
Pages 80–81

1. (2) The drug trade is destructive to all countries. Option (2) is correct because it is an opinion related to the information presented on the map. Options (1), (3), (4), and (5) are incorrect because the map shows them as facts, not opinions.

2. (5) Sanctions were not imposed on Mexico because it is a participant in NAFTA. Option (5) correctly identifies the implication suggested by the map that because Mexico is part of NAFTA, sanctions were not imposed. That there is more drug trade in Mexico than in Colombia (option 1) or more drug trade in Colombia than in Mexico (option 2) are both incorrect and are not implied by the map. The statements that sanctions were not imposed on Colombia because the country is farther from the U.S. (option 3) or that sanctions were imposed on Mexico because the country is closer to the U.S. (option 4) are both incorrect and not implied by the map.

3. (3) All European Union members use the Euro except Denmark, Sweden, and Britain, which retain their own national currencies. Option (3) is correct as indicated by the map title, which identifies part of the main idea, and the map key, which identifies the countries in yellow as using the Euro currency and the countries in blue–Britain, Denmark, and Sweden–as using national currencies. While it is true that Spain, France, and Germany use the Euro (option 1), this option does not include a reference to the other European Union countries on the map. Option (2) is an incomplete statement because Denmark should be included in this group. While it is correct that Sweden does not use the Euro (option 4), this is not the main idea of the map. Option (5) is incorrect because not all the major countries of Europe have implemented the Euro.

4. (5) major patterns of vegetation Option (5) is correct because the map clearly shows the types and locations of various types of vegetation. The map does not indicate the major agricultural products of Brazil (option 1), Brazil's population densities (option 2), the location of mountains and plateaus (option 3), or the location of mineral resources (option 4).

and plateaus (option 3), or the location of mineral resources (option 4).

5. **(2) Natal** Option (2) is correct because the map shows that the Natal region is in the Caatinga, or forests of thorny shrubs and stunted trees. This indicates it is a dry and inhospitable region and less desirable than others. The other options are incorrect because the equatorial forest region (option 1), Manaus (option 3), Cuiabá (option 4), and S. J. Campos (option 5) are probably more wet, hospitable, and desirable regions than that of Natal.

6. **(3) The Pantanal floods annually.** Option (3) is correct because the map indicates the area to the west of Cuiabá is the Pantanal (annually flooded lowland), which suggests this area has enough water to help support hydroelectric plants. Option (1) is incorrect because the equatorial forest does not seem to relate to hydroelectricity, and the map does not show the Amazon River. Option (2) is incorrect because whether or not the Caatinga has vegetation that does not need much water does not relate to placing hydroelectric plants in the region to the west of Cuiabá. The statements that tropical forests contain a rich abundance of wildlife (option 4) and the Cerrado supports agriculture (option 5) do not relate to placing hydroelectric plants in the region to the west of Cuiabá.

7. **(1) Brazil is not a highly developed country.** Option (1) is supported by the map, which shows that most of the country is covered with vegetation. Options (2) and (3) are incorrect because the map does not show the utilization of Brazil's natural resources. The map does not show the major cities of Brazil (option 4) or indicate the size of Brazil relative to that of the United States (option 5).

Skill 19 Combine Text and Graphics
Pages 84–85

1. **(3) The economy is experiencing a high rate of inflation.** Option (3) is correct based on the definition of inflation and the information in the cartoon, which shows a giant wallet needed to pay for only a few groceries. That goods such as groceries have become scarce (option 1), a good balance exists between prices and available goods (option 2), and the economy is experiencing a growth spurt (option 4) are incorrect and not implied by the passage or cartoon. While middle-class families may be hardest hit by inflation (option 5), this is not the best answer because it is an implication about consumers, not about the state of the economy.

2. **(1) freedom of speech** Option (1) is correct because it best relates to a candidate's effort to influence an election by spending his or her own funds. Nothing in the passage or chart suggests candidates spending their own funds relates to freedom of the press (option 2), trial by jury (option 3), privacy (option 4), or the right to petition the government (option 5).

3. **(3) Large contributions may improperly influence an elected official.** Option (3) is correct as implied by the passage, which states that campaign finance reform has been a concern, and the chart, which shows limiting individual contributions to a certain dollar amount—suggesting that large individual contributions could improperly influence an elected official. That the Supreme Court thinks money should be spent on social issues (option 1), money ensures the right candidate is elected (option 2), only the very wealthy can be elected

(option 4), or contributions should be given to charity instead of politics (option 5) are incorrect and not stated or suggested by the passage or chart.

4. **(1) It might serve to unify the country by connecting the Mississippi to the Pacific.** As stated in the passage, it was hoped that the Northwest Passage would extend from the Mississippi River to the Pacific Ocean (option 1). The other options are incorrect; that a Northwest Passage would encourage Congress to sell the Louisiana Purchase (option 2), politicians and business interests hoped a similar passage might be discovered in the Southeast (option 3), northeastern fur traders wanted to bring their wares to Portland (option 4), or European settlers in Portland wanted to take trips back east (option 5) are not supported by the passage or map.

5. **(2) It was located near the juncture of the Mississippi and Missouri Rivers.** Option (2) is correct because as the map shows, St. Louis is located near the intersection of the two major rivers, and the passage states the plan was to head up the Missouri to the Rocky Mountains. That St. Louis was on the same latitude as Washington, D.C. (option 1), is incorrect; the map doesn't indicate degrees of latitude. Neither the passage nor the map indicates that St. Louis was the capital of the Louisiana Purchase (option 3), a great railway center (option 4), or a center of learning and higher education (option 5).

6. **(3) There was only a short portage between the Missouri and Columbia Rivers.** Option (3) is correct because the passage notes that the party expected a "short portage" but suffered a difficult overland journey, making mistakes in direction and reaching dead ends en route to the Columbia River. While the party may have thought the Pacific was much closer (option 1), this is not the best answer because it doesn't address the problems of direction and finding a water passage that the party experienced. Option (2) is incorrect because nothing indicates that they believed this. Option (4) is incorrect because, as the passage implies, there was no map of the Northwest before Lewis and Clark's expedition. Option (5) is incorrect because neither the map nor the passage indicates that Louisiana bordered on the Pacific Ocean.

Skill 20 Combine Information from
Graphics Pages 88–89

1. **(1) higher prices** Option (1) correctly identifies the variable on the supply curve that causes output to rise. The statement that lower prices (option 2) cause output to rise is opposite the correct answer. Larger output (option 3) is incorrect because this is another way to refer to output that increases, or goes up; it can't cause itself. Smaller output (option 4) is incorrect because it refers to output that decreases, or goes down, and doesn't address the causes of rising output. The statement that lower prices and larger output (option 5) cause output to rise is incorrect because lower prices is opposite the correct answer and larger output is another way to refer to output that increases, or goes up.

2. **(4) lower prices** Option (4) is correct; as the demand curve shows, the number of shoes bought (demand) goes

answer. Options (2) and (3) are incorrect because greater and decreasing supply are shown on the supply curve, and this question refers only to the demand curve. Option (5) is incorrect. Higher prices, as noted, is opposite the correct answer, and larger supply is not shown on the demand curve.

3. **(3) large supply and low demand** Option (3) is correct; based on the demand curve, as prices go down, demand increases. A retailer selling shoes might make the decision to lower prices based on having plenty of shoes in stock and the desire to increase demand in order to sell that inventory. Having a small supply and high demand (option 1) would probably cause a retailer to raise prices. Having a small supply alone (option 2) or large demand alone (option 4) are incorrect and opposite the correct answer as noted. Option (5) is incorrect because having a high demand for an item means the retailer probably does not need to lower prices.

4. **(5) Both (3) and (4).** Option (5) is correct because it best combines information shown in the graphs. Producers can reach the largest output when selling prices are their highest. Consumers will buy the most products when they are priced at their lowest. While it's true that the less a product costs, the more of it consumers will want to buy (option 1) and consumers want to buy as many products as possible at the lowest possible prices (option 4), these are not the best answers because they don't make any assumptions about producers' motives and preferences. Option (2) is incorrect because according to the demand curve, the more a product costs, the less consumers will buy. While it is true that producers want to make as many products as they can, and to sell those products at the highest possible prices (option 3), this is not the best answer because it doesn't address consumers' motives and preferences.

5. **(4) The legislative process is complicated and can take a long time to complete.** Option (4) is correct because it is supported by the flowchart, which shows the complex path a bill must follow from its original introduction until its signing into law by the president of the United States. It is also supported by information in the table, which indicates the legislative process is slow moving. The statement that a bill may be drafted by a committee in the House of Representatives (option 1) is contradicted by the flowchart, which shows that the House committee would be responsible for approving, amending, or pigeonholing a bill. The statement a bill may be submitted by the president if the House and Senate agree (option 2) is contradicted by the table, which says it is fact that one must be a member of Congress to submit a bill and fiction that the president can submit bills. The statement that a bill does not have to go through the entire legislative process if it is approved in the initial hearings (option 3) is contradicted by the flowchart, which shows a bill approved in initial hearings in either the House or Senate must continue on to committee action. The statement that the legislative process should be changed to reflect current needs of the U.S. (option 5) is incorrect because this is not a logical assumption but an opinion about the process.

6. **(2) during floor action** A bill is likely to receive the closest attention when it is in floor action (option 2) because this is the point at which a bill is either passed, sent back to committee, amended, or killed. While committee action (option 1) is critical to a bill's moving forward or not, this is not the best answer because a bill can be expected to be analyzed even more thoroughly during floor action, as noted. Option (3) is incorrect because there is no conference committee between the House and Senate. Option (4) is not the best answer because when the president approves or vetoes a bill, it has already gone through scrutiny by many other people and committees, and the president likely already has a strong opinion about which course of action he or she will take. Option (5) is incorrect because bills are discussed at many points in the process. Most debate happens during floor action.

Pretest Answer Sheet: Social Studies

Name: _____ Class: _____ Date: _____

1 ①②③④⑤	5 ①②③④⑤	9 ①②③④⑤	13 ①②③④⑤	17 ①②③④⑤
2 ①②③④⑤	6 ①②③④⑤	10 ①②③④⑤	14 ①②③④⑤	18 ①②③④⑤
3 ①②③④⑤	7 ①②③④⑤	11 ①②③④⑤	15 ①②③④⑤	19 ①②③④⑤
4 ①②③④⑤	8 ①②③④⑤	12 ①②③④⑤	16 ①②③④⑤	20 ①②③④⑤

Official GED Practice Test Form PA Answer Sheet: Social Studies

Name: ______________________ Class: __________ Date: __________

Time Started: __________

Time Finished: __________

1 ①②③④⑤	6 ①②③④⑤	11 ①②③④⑤	16 ①②③④⑤	21 ①②③④⑤
2 ①②③④⑤	7 ①②③④⑤	12 ①②③④⑤	17 ①②③④⑤	22 ①②③④⑤
3 ①②③④⑤	8 ①②③④⑤	13 ①②③④⑤	18 ①②③④⑤	23 ①②③④⑤
4 ①②③④⑤	9 ①②③④⑤	14 ①②③④⑤	19 ①②③④⑤	24 ①②③④⑤
5 ①②③④⑤	10 ①②③④⑤	15 ①②③④⑤	20 ①②③④⑤	25 ①②③④⑤